National Security Consequences of U.S. Oil Dependency

National Security Consequences of U.S. Oil Dependency

Report of an Independent Task Force

Sponsored by the Council on Foreign Relations

Founded in 1921, the Council on Foreign Relations is an independent, national membership organization and a nonpartisan center for scholars dedicated to producing and disseminating ideas so that individual and corporate members, as well as policymakers, journalists, students, and interested citizens in the United States and other countries, can better understand the world and the foreign policy choices facing the United States and other governments. The Council does this by convening meetings; conducting a wide-ranging Studies program; publishing *Foreign Affairs*, the preeminent journal covering international affairs and U.S. foreign policy; maintaining a diverse membership; sponsoring Independent Task Forces; and providing up-to-date information about the world and U.S. foreign policy on the Council's website, www.cfr.org.

THE COUNCIL TAKES NO INSTITUTIONAL POSITION ON POLICY ISSUES AND HAS NO AFFILIATION WITH THE U.S. GOVERNMENT. ALL STATEMENTS OF FACT AND EXPRESSIONS OF OPINION CONTAINED IN ITS PUBLICA-TIONS ARE THE SOLE RESPONSIBILITY OF THE AUTHOR OR AUTHORS.

The Council will sponsor an Independent Task Force when (1) an issue of current and critical importance to U.S. foreign policy arises, and (2) it seems that a group diverse in backgrounds and perspectives may, nonetheless, be able to reach a meaningful consensus on a policy through private and nonpartisan deliberations. Typically, a Task Force meets between two and five times over a brief period to ensure the relevance of its work.

Upon reaching a conclusion, a Task Force issues a report, and the Council publishes its text and posts it on the Council website. Task Force reports reflect a strong and meaningful policy consensus, with Task Force members endorsing the general policy thrust and judgments reached by the group, though not necessarily every finding and recommendation. Task Force members who join the consensus may submit additional or dissenting views, which are included in the final report. "Chairman's Reports" are signed by Task Force chairs only and are usually preceded or followed by full Task Force reports. Upon reaching a conclusion, a Task Force may also ask individuals who were not members of the Task Force to associate themselves with the Task Force report to enhance its impact. All Task Force reports "benchmark" their findings against current administration policy to make explicit areas of agreement and disagreement. The Task Force is solely responsible for its report. The Council takes no institutional position.

For further information about the Council or this Independent Task Force, please write to the Council on Foreign Relations, 58 East 68th Street, New York, NY 10021, or call the Communications office at 212-434-9888. Visit our website at www.cfr.org.

Task Force Chairs

John Deutch

John Deutch

James R. Schlesinger

James R. Schlesinger

Project Director

David G. Victor

David G. Victor

Task Force Members

Graham T. Allison

Norman R. Augustine

Robert A. Belfer

Stephen W. Bosworth

Helima L. Croft

John Deutch

Charles J. DiBona

Jessica P. Einhorn

Martin S. Feldstein

David L. Goldwyn*

Michael D. Granoff*

J. Bennett Johnston

Arnold Kanter

Karin M. Lissakers

Walter E. Massey

Ernest J. Moniz

William K. Reilly

James R. Schlesinger

Peter Schwartz

Philip R. Sharp

James B. Steinberg

Linda G. Stuntz

James L. Sweeney

Frank Verrastro

David G. Victor

J. Robinson West

*The individual has endorsed the report and submitted an additional view.

Contents

Foreword

Through most of the 1990s energy supplies were plentiful and prices were low. *The Economist* speculated about the political consequences of a world in which oil declined to $5 per barrel. U.S. foreign policy generally accorded little attention to energy, except in special circumstances such as the location of strategic pipelines in Central Asia.

In recent years, energy prices have surged. President George W. Bush, in this year's State of the Union address, warned of an addiction to imported oil and its perils. Yet there is no consensus on what should be done to shake the addiction. Virtually everything concerning energy has changed—except U.S. policy.

The Council on Foreign Relations established an Independent Task Force to examine the consequences of dependence on imported energy for U.S. foreign policy. Since the United States both consumes and imports more oil than any other country, the Task Force has concentrated its deliberations on matters of petroleum. In so doing, it reaches a sobering but inescapable judgment: the lack of sustained attention to energy issues is undercutting U.S. foreign policy and national security.

The Task Force goes on to argue that U.S. energy policy has been plagued by myths, such as the feasibility of achieving "energy independence" through increased drilling or anything else. For the next few decades, the challenge facing the United States is to become better equipped to manage its dependencies rather than pursue the chimera of independence.

The issues at stake intimately affect U.S. foreign policy, as well as the strength of the American economy and the state of the global environment. But most of the leverage potentially available to the United States is through domestic policy. Thus, the Independent Task Force devotes considerable attention to how oil consumption (or at least the growth in consumption) can be reduced and why and how energy issues must become better integrated with other aspects of U.S. foreign policy.

The Council is indebted to John Deutch and James R. Schlesinger, two prominent Americans with long and distinguished records of public service, for chairing this important group. The Council is also grateful to the members of the Task Force for volunteering their time and efforts over ten months to the project. I also wish to thank David G. Victor, adjunct senior fellow at the Council, for so ably and professionally directing the enterprise.

Richard N. Haass
President
Council on Foreign Relations
October 2006

Acknowledgments

The Independent Task Force on Energy and U.S. Foreign Policy, sponsored by the Council on Foreign Relations, was privileged to have two distinguished leaders, John Deutch and James R. Schlesinger, as its chairs. From the original conception of the study through the final editing, both have been closely engaged with the process, and the end product has benefited tremendously from their experience and pragmatism. I am very grateful for the opportunity to work with them and with the diverse and thoughtful membership of the whole Task Force.

The Task Force was fortunate to depend on Lee Feinstein, executive director of the Council's Task Force program, and his deputy, Lindsay Workman, who closely guided us through the entire process of meetings, drafting, and marketing. Divya Reddy, the research associate for the Task Force, skillfully organized meetings, kept numerous drafts and endless edits in order, and kept the entire enterprise on track with grace and uncommon skill. We thank her, especially.

Other Council colleagues have been generous with their time and talent. Leigh Gusts and the Council's library staff helped us create a website for the project and organized diverse sources of data and background material. Mark Bucknam, a colonel with the U.S. Air Force who visited the Council during 2005–2006, helped with every aspect of our effort, notably with background research and the compilation of extremely useful factual charts on energy trends. Irina Faskianos, David Kellogg, Nancy Roman, Lisa Shields, and Anya Schmemann guided an impressive outreach effort, while Patricia Dorff and Molly Graham oversaw all aspects of publication.

We greatly appreciate the efforts of Rachel Bronson who, along with several other Task Force members, briefed us at one of our meetings about patterns of investment and political stability in major oil-producing regions. Our recommendations benefited from presentations of our midcourse findings to special Council audiences in New York, San Francisco, and Washington, DC. We also thank Assheton Carter, Ian Gary, Corinna Gilfillan, Sherri W. Goodman, David Hawkins, Lee Lane, Nigel Purvis, Daniel K. Tarullo, and Timothy E. Wirth, who advised us on ways to address links to environmental policy and the varied attempts to improve governance in oil-rich countries. Philip K. Verleger Jr. helped us understand how shifts in the way that oil markets operate can affect the need for and operation of the strategic petroleum reserve. Michelle N. Billig, Charles D. Ferguson, Douglas Holtz-Eakin, Princeton N. Lyman, William A. Pizer, and Stephen Sestanovich provided useful background materials and discussions on a variety of topics addressed in the report.

The Task Force would like to extend a special thanks to Richard N. Haass, president of the Council on Foreign Relations, for calling for a policy review on energy matters in these challenging times. In convening the Task Force, Richard relied, in part, on the results of a very useful scoping meeting in August 2005 attended by Rachel Bronson, Kimball C. Chen, Richard Herold, Ira B. Joseph, Edward L. Morse, Rodney W. Nichols, David Nissen, and Vijay V. Vaitheeswaran.

Finally, the Council on Foreign Relations expresses thanks to Washington and Lee University and the Lenfest Foundation, as well as the many individual Council members who have generously supported this specific Task Force and the work of the Task Force program more generally.

David G. Victor
Project Director

Task Force Report

Overview and Introduction

The lack of sustained attention to energy issues is undercutting U.S. foreign policy and U.S. national security. Major energy suppliers—from Russia to Iran to Venezuela—have been increasingly able and willing to use their energy resources to pursue their strategic and political objectives. Major energy consumers—notably the United States, but other countries as well—are finding that their growing dependence on imported energy increases their strategic vulnerability and constrains their ability to pursue a broad range of foreign policy and national security objectives. Dependence also puts the United States into increasing competition with other importing countries, notably with today's rapidly growing emerging economies of China and India. At best, these trends will challenge U.S. foreign policy; at worst, they will seriously strain relations between the United States and these countries.

This report focuses on the foreign policy issues that arise from dependence on energy traded in world markets and outlines a strategy for response. And because U.S. reliance on the global market for oil, much of which comes from politically unstable parts of the world, is greater than for any other primary energy source, this report is mainly about oil. To a lesser degree it also addresses natural gas.

Put simply, the reliable and affordable supply of energy—"energy security"—is an increasingly prominent feature of the international political landscape and bears on the effectiveness of U.S. foreign policy. At the same time, however, the United States has largely continued to treat "energy policy" as something that is separate and distinct—

3

substantively and organizationally—from "foreign policy." This must change. The United States needs not merely to coordinate but to integrate energy issues with its foreign policy.

The challenge over the next several decades is to manage the consequences of unavoidable dependence on oil and gas that is traded in world markets and to begin the transition to an economy that relies less on petroleum. The longer the delay, the greater will be the subsequent trauma. For the United States, with 4.6 percent of the world's population using 25 percent of the world's oil, the transition could be especially disruptive.

This report concentrates on the next twenty years, a period long enough to put necessary policy measures into place but not so distant as to encounter a wider range of future geopolitical or technological uncertainties. During this next twenty years (and quite probably beyond), it is infeasible to eliminate the nation's dependence on foreign energy sources. The voices that espouse "energy independence" are doing the nation a disservice by focusing on a goal that is unachievable over the foreseeable future and that encourages the adoption of inefficient and counterproductive policies. Indeed, during the next two decades, it is unlikely that the United States will be able to make a sharp reduction in its dependence on imports, which currently stand at 60 percent of consumption. The central task for the next two decades must be to manage the consequences of dependence on oil, not to pretend the United States can eliminate it.

A popular response to the steep rise in energy prices in recent years is the false expectation that policies to lower imports will automatically lead to a decline in prices. The public's continuing expectation of the availability of cheap energy alternatives will almost surely be disappointed. While oil prices may retreat from their current high levels, one should not expect the price of oil to return, on a sustained basis, to the low levels seen in the late 1990s. In fact, if more costly domestic supply is used to substitute for imported oil, then prices will not moderate. Yet the public's elected representatives have allowed this myth to survive, as they advocate policies that futilely attempt to reduce import dependence quickly while simultaneously lowering prices. Leaders of both political parties, especially when seeking public office, seem unable to resist announcing unrealistic goals that are transparent efforts to gain popularity rather than inform the public of the challenges the United States must overcome. Moreover, the political system of the United States has so far proved unable to sustain the policies that would be needed to manage dependence on imported fuels. As history since 1973 shows, the call for policy action recedes as prices abate.

These problems rooted in the dependence on oil are neither new nor unique to the United States. Other major world economies that rely on imported oil—from Western Europe to Japan, and now China and India—face similar concerns. All are having difficulties in meeting the challenges of managing demand for oil. But these countries do not share the foreign policy responsibilities of the United States. And the United States, insufficiently aware of its vulnerability, has not been as attentive as the other large industrialized countries in implementing policies to slow the rising demand for oil. Yet even if the United States were self-sufficient in oil (a condition the Task Force considers wholly infeasible in the foreseeable future), U.S. foreign policy would remain constrained as long as U.S. allies and partners remained dependent on imports because of their mutual interdependence. Thus, while reducing U.S. oil imports is desirable, the underlying problem is the high and growing demand for oil worldwide.

The growing worldwide demand for oil in the coming decades will magnify the problems that are already evident in the functioning of the world oil market. During that period, the availability of low-cost oil resources is expected to decline; production and transportation costs are likely to rise. As more hydrocarbon resources in more remote areas are tapped, the world economy will become even more dependent on elaborate and vulnerable infrastructures to bring oil and gas to the markets where they are used.

For the last three decades, the United States has correctly followed a policy strategy that, in large measure, has stressed the importance of markets. Energy markets, however, do not operate in an economically perfect and transparent manner. For example, the Organization of Petroleum Exporting Countries (OPEC), quite notably, seeks to act as a cartel. Most oil and gas resources are controlled by state-run companies, some of which enter into supply contracts with consumer countries that are accompanied by political arrangements that distort the proper functioning of the market. These agreements, such as those spearheaded by the Chinese government in oil-rich countries across Africa and elsewhere, reflect many intentions, including the desire to "lock up" particular supplies for the Chinese market. Some of the state companies that control these resources are inefficient, which imposes further costs on the world market. And some governments use the revenues from hydrocarbon sales for political purposes that harm U.S. interests. Because of these realities, an active public policy is needed to correct these market failures that harm U.S. economic and national security. The market will not automatically deliver the best outcome.

The Task Force recommends a policy strategy based on five types of actions.

First, while the United States has limited leverage to achieve its energy security objectives through foreign policy actions, it has considerable ability to manage its energy future through the adoption of domestic policies that complement both a short- and long-term international strategy.

The Task Force is unanimous in recommending the adoption of incentives to slow and eventually reverse the growth in consumption of petroleum products, especially transportation fuels such as motor gasoline. However, the Task Force did not agree about the particular options that would best achieve this objective. The Task Force considered three measures:

- A tax on gasoline (with the tax revenue recycled into the economy with a fraction possibly earmarked for specific purposes such as financing of energy technology research and development [R&D]);
- Stricter and broader mandated Corporate Average Fuel Economy standards, known as CAFE standards; and
- The use of tradable gasoline permits that would cap the total level of gasoline consumed in the economy.

Used singly or in combination, these measures would not only encourage higher-efficiency vehicles (although these will take time to find their way into the fleet), but also encourage the introduction of alternative fuels, as well as promote changes in behavior such as the greater use of public transportation. While there are other domestic policies that could be adopted to limit demand for fuels, no strategy will be effective without higher prices for transportation fuels or regulatory incentives to use more efficient vehicles.

The Task Force does not believe there is a corresponding need to adopt additional measures to limit demand for natural gas. While there are reasons to be concerned about the adequacy of the near-term supply of natural gas to the North American market, at present natural gas markets work relatively well. To date, there is little dependence on natural gas from outside of North America, thus avoiding the political repercussions accompanying oil imports.

There are large amounts of "stranded" gas available around the world that can be transported to markets using technologies that are increasingly economic. Most attention is focused on the technologies of liquefied natural gas (LNG), through which gas is cooled and compressed to a liquid, shipped on tankers, and then warmed and re-gasified to its original form. Realizing the potential for LNG will require additional facilities to receive and re-gasify imported LNG in the United States.

At the same time that the United States promotes measures to reduce oil demand, it should also be prepared to open some new areas for exploration and production of oil and gas, for example, in Alaska, along the East and West coasts, and in the Gulf of Mexico. In addition to modestly increasing supply, encouraging domestic production is a valuable, if not essential, element for increasing the credibility of U.S. efforts to persuade other nations to expand their exploration and production activities.

Ultimately, technology will be vital to reducing the dependence on oil and gas, and to making a transition away from petroleum fuels. These benefits of improved technology will come in the future only if investments are made today in research, development, and demonstration (RD&D).

The Task Force notes that higher energy prices are unleashing remarkable forces for innovation in this country. Entrepreneurs are seeking new ideas for products and services, such as batteries, fuel cells, and biofuels. Private equity capital is seeking opportunities to invest in new energy technologies. Large corporations are investing in RD&D in all aspects of energy production and use. These activities will undoubtedly result in a steady improvement in the ability of the U.S. economy to meet energy needs.

The U.S. government has an important role in supporting this innovation in the private sector, especially for technologies that require significant development efforts to demonstrate commercial potential. The Task Force recommends that the federal government offer greatly expanded incentives and investments aimed at both short- and long-term results to address a wide range of technologies that includes higher-efficiency vehicles, substitutes for oil in transportation (such as biomass and electricity), techniques to enhance production from existing oil wells, and technologies that increase the energy efficiency of industrial processes that use oil and gas. Government spending is appropriate in this context because the market alone does not make as much effort as is warranted by national security and environmental considerations.

Second, we recommend that the United States take several initiatives to encourage the efficient, transparent, and fair operation of world oil and gas markets. The United States must not act alone in this endeavor, as all consumer nations have a common interest in well-functioning international markets for oil and gas.

The United States should continue to urge governments in all countries to reduce subsidies and deregulate the prices of oil and gas where they have been held below world market levels. While progress has been made over the last three decades, many countries—notably large developing countries, such as China, and large energy producers, such as Saudi Arabia and Venezuela—still regulate and subsidize their consumption of fuel. Russia, among many other gas-rich countries, still subsidizes its internal consumption of natural gas. These arrangements result in a world market that is not properly responsive to underlying supply and demand.

The United States should also take the lead in revising cooperative agreements originally reached in the International Energy Agency (IEA) in the early 1970s. These agreements require their members to maintain adequate national oil stockpiles and to follow procedures for coping with shortages in case of a disruption in supply. The most important revision would find a mechanism to include the large, rapidly growing economies, notably China and India, so that they can build adequate strategic reserves and coordinate the use of those reserves with other major oil importers. The best approach would involve expanding the IEA. However, an alternative institution, such as a greatly strengthened International Energy Forum (IEF), could also serve this purpose.[1]

The United States should remove the protectionist tariff on imported ethanol, as that makes it much harder for U.S. refineries to take advantage of efficient ethanol producers outside our borders, such as in Brazil.

The executive branch and Congress should also reexamine the management of the United States' strategic stockpiles and consider whether the procedures for using these stockpiles should be updated so that they are more consistent with today's realities, such as the presence of large private stockpiles and strong oil and gas futures markets.

Third, producing and consuming countries have a common interest in reducing infrastructure vulnerability, whether to terrorist attacks or natural disasters. In the last year alone, there has been one attempted major attack on the Saudi oil processing facility at Abqaiq, and hurricanes Katrina and Rita caused substantial damage to oil and gas processing and transport infrastructure in the United States. The United States must work more closely with major oil suppliers, notably Saudi Arabia, to detect and deter attacks on their infrastructure. Greater efforts are needed to harden the energy infrastructure against both attacks and natural disasters. Over the coming decades the importance of these infrastructures is likely to grow as low-cost oil resources close at hand are depleted and hydrocarbon resources in more remote areas are tapped.

Fourth, there are too many examples of countries that exploit their oil and natural gas resources while failing to manage the revenues in a way that improves the social and economic prospects of their people. While there are limits to what can be accomplished, the Task Force believes the United States must play a stronger role in promoting better management of hydrocarbon revenues. Too often, these revenues accrue to a small minority that is unaccountable to any representative political authority, which not only undermines governance, but also

---

[1] The IEF was established in 2003 as a ministerial-level dialogue between major energy producers and consumers.

e political stability that is essential to reliable production of oil and gas. Such actions are in the U.S. interest, both because stably governed countries are better able to attract the investment needed to maintain and increase hydrocarbon production, and because it supports the long-standing American goal of encouraging progress toward democracy and good governance.

Most proposals for better management of hydrocarbon revenues rely on encouraging investors and governments to disclose payments and improve accounting, on the theory that greater transparency will make it easier to detect corruption, encourage better spending of revenues, and generally lead to better governance. Most notable of these is an initiative by the British government, working through international institutions, to implement the Extractive Industries Transparency Initiative (EITI). Making such schemes work is very difficult because, while voluntary, they can be seen as intrusions on a nation's sovereign prerogative to manage its own revenues. Yet there are encouraging signs—such as efforts in Azerbaijan, Kazakhstan, and Nigeria to apply the EITI's accounting standards—that these systems have a significant and positive effect. The United States should play a more active role in promoting the use of these mechanisms through its own actions and by working to convince others, such as the governments in China and India, of the importance of these measures.

Fifth, the U.S. government is not well organized to address the threats to national security created by energy dependence. There is a need to mobilize the resources of the government in a manner that better ensures continuity of attention and integration of the political, economic, technical, and security perspectives needed for energy policy-making. Closer attention to organization is needed mainly in the executive branch, but complementary actions by Congress, through legislation and hearings, will also be needed.

The success of any prescription to integrate energy issues into the foreign policy process is made difficult by the enormous range of other issues that demand the attention of high-level policymakers. The Task Force recommends that a small energy security directorate be established within the National Security Staff to coordinate interagency policymaking on energy security issues. It also recommends that the secretary of energy be engaged in any foreign policy deliberations that involve energy issues. In addition, the Task Force suggests that the terms of reference of all planning studies at the National Security Council (NSC), Department of Defense, Department of State, and the intelligence community include energy security considerations. The Task Force cautions that it would be neither practical nor wise to insist that energy security be the central foreign policy priority of the United States.

Scope of the Task Force's Inquiry

The Task Force has restricted its inquiry to the challenges of managing U.S. and global dependence on imported oil and gas. This focus necessarily means that it has not addressed other important energy security subjects.

One example is nuclear proliferation. The Task Force believes for many reasons that the world will need more nuclear power in the future. However, a significant increase in the number of nuclear power plants and their associated fuel cycle could also pose risks to the proliferation of nuclear weapons. Iran is a vivid example today. It is important to work toward an international system that prevents the spread of potentially dangerous fuel cycle facilities while, at the same time, assuring a reliable supply of nuclear fuel for countries that build commercial power reactors.

We also have not addressed the important and complex foreign policy issues surrounding global warming, an issue that will be prominent on the foreign policy agenda in coming years, and which the Council has addressed in an earlier publication.[2] A sober judgment on the best policy for the United States to pursue requires examining a number of factors, including the state of scientific knowledge about global warming, the costs and benefits of different carbon emission control mechanisms, and the timing of adoption of possible policies by other countries, including the rapidly growing developing economies. The Task Force did not address these issues in depth nor did it make specific recommendations, but it has considered global warming in its

---

[2] David G. Victor, *Climate Change: Debating America's Policy Options* (New York: Council on Foreign Relations Press, 2004).

deliberations. In particular, policies intended to reduce demand for fossil fuels—such as those advocated here—can also slow the accumulation of gases that contribute to global warming.

Findings: The U.S. Energy System and the Role of Imported Oil and Gas

Energy comes to the U.S. economy from various primary sources. Oil and gas, the two primary energy sources that are imported in substantial quantities, supply about 63 percent (figure 1). The third of the largest sources of primary energy, coal, is available from abundant domestic sources. The remaining sources are nuclear power, biomass (wood waste and biofuels), hydroelectric power, and geothermal, solar, and wind power.

Most (68 percent) of the oil used in the United States is for transportation, and oil fuels 96 percent of transportation needs.[3] This domination of oil in the transportation sector is the result of its relatively low cost over most of history, and its convenience as a high-energy-density liquid that is easy to store and transport. It is the dependence of the transportation system on liquid fuel that makes oil so important in the U.S. economy.

Natural gas, in contrast to oil, is more evenly split among end uses. In the 1990s, the high efficiency and low capital cost of natural gas-fired electricity-generating plants, coupled with the low price of natural

---

[3] The remaining supply comes from natural gas, alcohol fuels produced mainly from corn, and small amounts of electricity.

gas, made this clean fuel the preferred choice for new electricity generation plants. But as natural gas prices have increased roughly threefold, pulverized coal-fired steam-generating power plants have returned to favor despite concerns about their carbon dioxide (CO_2) emissions. In contrast to oil, domestic energy sources, such as coal, can substitute for natural gas use.

Myth #1: The United States can be energy independent.

No, because liquid fuels are essential to the nation's transportation system. Barring draconian measures, the United States will depend on imported oil for a significant fraction of its transportation fuel needs for at least several decades.

Oil Supply and Demand

Over the last fifty years, U.S. consumption of oil has grown continually, except for a time during the late 1970s and early 1980s.[4] Whereas consumption has generally risen, ever since the early 1970s, U.S. oil production in the lower forty-eight states has been in decline (figure 2). As a result, net imports of oil—which is imported mainly as crude but also refined products such as gasoline—increased steadily through 1977, declined from then until 1982, and have been growing ever since.[5] U.S. policymakers became alarmed in the 1970s as U.S. imports rose to 50 percent and sought successfully to reduce demand and thus imports to about one-third of its consumption. Today, despite these efforts, import dependence is roughly 60 percent and expected to rise during the coming decades.[6]

---

[4] During this brief period, a combination of CAFE standards and increased oil prices temporarily reduced demand through higher fuel efficiency and also by switching from oil to other fuels, such as in the generation of electric power.

[5] The country of origin of oil imported into the United States—currently Canada, Mexico, Saudi Arabia, Venezuela, and Nigeria are the largest suppliers—depends on many factors, including the cost of transportation and the quality of the oil. However, the exact origin of the imported oil is not particularly significant to its market impact since the global oil market rapidly adjusts to match buyers and sellers. What matters is the total global balance of demand and supply and the trends in total production and consumption.

[6] The U.S. Department of Energy's EIA *Annual Energy Outlook 2006* reference case projections estimate that, for the United States, imports will grow from 58.4 percent of the 20.74 million barrels per day oil consumption in 2004 to 62.3 percent of the 27.7 million barrels per day oil consumption in 2030.

Figure 1: U.S. Primary Energy Consumption by Source, 2005

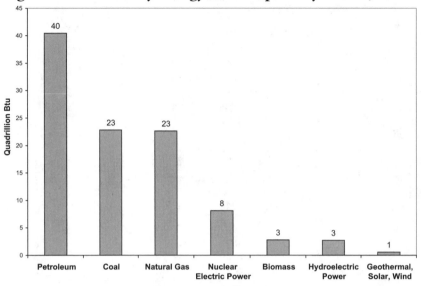

Source: Energy Information Administration (EIA), *Annual Energy Review 2005.*

After rapid price increases in 1973 and later in 1979–81, nominal U.S. prices of crude oil dropped significantly in the early 1980s. Adjusted for inflation, real oil prices dropped even more rapidly. As a result, the United States and other oil consumers enjoyed a period from 1986 through 2004 of relatively stable and low prices. Since then the price of benchmark crude oils has grown.

The price of crude oil in the United States reflects the price in the world oil market, which depends on conditions of global supply and demand. The sharp increase in oil prices over the past two years has been the result of supply and demand forces: the worldwide demand for oil has grown, notably in the United States and in China, while oil production capacity has not risen as rapidly (figure 4). This situation is exacerbated by stiffer environmental standards, such as rules that require refineries to make products with lower sulfur content. New refinery capacity has lagged, and some existing refineries cannot handle the heavier oil with higher sulfur that is offered in the market, which requires more processing to be upgraded into useful refined products.

Figure 2: U.S. Consumption, Production, and Imports of Oil, 1949–2005

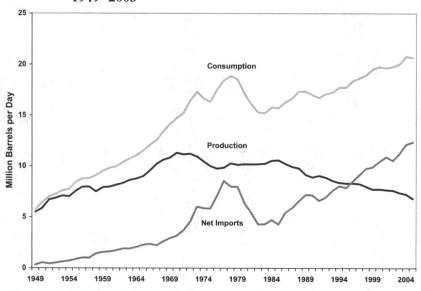

Source: EIA, *Annual Energy Review 2005.*

At times, oil prices also reflect the actions of the oil cartel OPEC. During times that the OPEC nations have held large amounts of extra capacity available for production, OPEC has been able to approximately stabilize the oil price, keeping it from dropping to the very low level that would reflect true market competition. This has been accomplished by an imperfectly observed agreement among the OPEC members to limit their production of crude oil and possibly through limitations on investments in oil production capacity. At times like now when there is very little extra capacity, the OPEC cartel has little or no ability to keep prices from rising. The potential market power of OPEC will not decline in future years, partly because the market share of oil production by OPEC is not expected to decline.[7]

---

[7] The situation is vividly illustrated by the EIA *International Energy Outlook (IEO–2006)* reference case projection that total world oil consumption will increase from 80.1 million barrels of oil per day (MMBD) in 2003 to 118.0 MMBD in 2030 with OPEC's conventional oil share of supply estimated to grow slightly from 38.5 percent today to about 40 percent; unconventional oil production is estimated to account for less than 10 percent of the 2030 total. Many members of the Task Force are skeptical that either of these high production estimates for 2030 will be achieved.

Figure 3: Nominal and Real Refiner Acquisition Costs (RAC)★ of Crude Oil

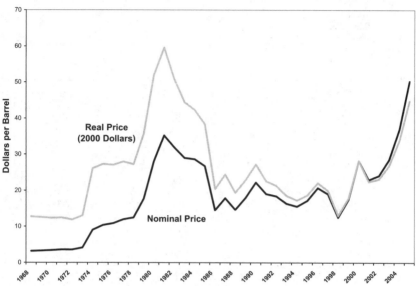

★RAC is the average cost of crude oil acquired by refineries in the United States.
Source: EIA, *Annual Energy Review 2005.*

Myth #2: Cutting oil imports will lower fuel prices.

Probably not. If policies aimed at cutting imports also reduce demand for fuel, then prices in the world market may decline. However, policies that mandate reduction of imports while demand stays high will force some consumers to turn to higher-priced substitutes to meet their needs.

When there is very little extra production capacity, as may be likely over the foreseeable future, small shifts in the worldwide supply and demand for oil can have significant impacts on the world market. That is because the demand for oil varies little with price, at least over short periods of time. Thus, for example, in today's tight market a 1 percent increase in world oil consumption (0.85 million barrels per day), or a similar decline in supply, can be expected to increase world oil prices by between 5 percent and 10 percent ($3.50 to $7 per barrel, at current prices).[8]

---

[8] This estimate assumes a short-run elasticity of demand between -0.1 and -0.2 and no immediate changes in supply in response to new prices. "Elasticity" is the fraction change in

Figure 4: Annual Growth in World Oil Demand

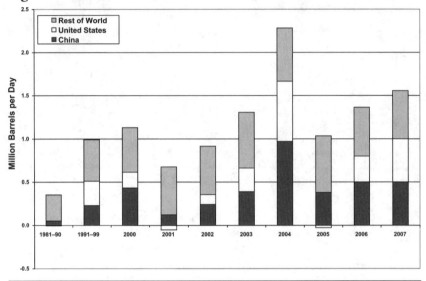

Source: EIA, *Short-Term Energy Outlook,* February 2006 (1981–90 and 1991–99 are annual averages).

Over a period of several years, the production capacity in the world oil market can change in response to economic conditions, including oil price. Higher prices create an incentive for more production, reduced demand, and innovation for substitutes.

Over the last few decades the trend has been for major resource holders to rely to a greater extent on national oil companies (NOCs) to manage their oil and gas production. In recent years, with high prices, some countries such as Russia and Venezuela have increased the authority of these state companies. NOCs control some three-quarters of the world's oil reserves. Indeed, the largest independent oil company, Exxon Mobil, ranks only fourteenth on the list of proven reserve owners, behind a long list of NOCs.

demand in response to a change in price. The small negative value indicates that, in the short term, when prices rise there is only a small decline in consumption of oil products. The elasticity values used here, which are typical, are estimated by Task Force members based on extensive published literature.

Myth #3: *Large Western companies like Exxon Mobil, BP, Shell, and Chevron control the price of oil.*

No, the resources and production controlled by large international oil companies are small compared with the NOCs. The pace of increasing extraction of hydrocarbons probably rests largely with NOCs, many of which are not governed solely by economic considerations. The international major companies control only about one-tenth of the world's proven hydrocarbon resources.

The presence of NOCs is important because many NOCs do not respond to market forces as would a private, competitive firm. In some circumstances this can benefit consumers, including U.S. consumers. For example, for many years, Saudi Aramco has maintained excess capacity that has helped to stabilize the world market. In other cases, however, the NOCs have constrained supply for longer than needed because these companies have either chosen to limit their production levels in order to support prices or have had difficulty attracting the capital and technology needed to maintain and expand output. Some NOCs, often because of domestic political influences, are inefficient, such as Mexico's Pemex and, now, Venezuela's PDVSA following President Hugo Chávez's coming into power and stripping the company of much of its expertise. Other NOCs, such as Saudi Aramco and Brazil's Petrobras, are more efficient. Investment decisions on actions to increase production by an NOC can be less responsive to market price signals than an investor-owned international oil company (IOC). The basic pattern of resource ownership and production control between IOCs and NOCs is unlikely to change appreciably—or at least not under the influence of U.S. policy—as many oil-rich countries have decided to vest control over their natural resources in state enterprises. However, there is some potential to improve efficiency by assisting those that welcome reforms in management and operations.

The high price of oil imposes real costs on the U.S. economy, lowering the living standard of American households. A $25 per barrel price rise reduces real income by about 1 percent of gross domestic product (GDP). In addition, the payments for oil lead to large dollar balances built up by oil producers, "petrodollars," giving them potential

Table 1: World Proved Oil Reserves by Country as of January 1, 2006 (billion barrels)

Country	Oil Reserves
Saudi Arabia	264.3
Canada	178.8
Iran	132.5
Iraq	115.0
Kuwait	101.5
United Arab Emirates	97.8
Venezuela	79.7
Russia	60.0
Libya	39.1
Nigeria	35.9
United States	21.4
China	18.3
Qatar	15.2
Mexico	12.9
Algeria	11.4
Brazil	11.2
Kazakhstan	9.0
Norway	7.7
Azerbaijan	7.0
India	5.8
Rest of World	68.1
World Total	*1,292.5*

Source: "Worldwide Look at Reserves and Production," *Oil & Gas Journal* 103: 47 (December 19, 2005), pp. 24–25.

leverage over U.S. capital markets.[9] Our concern is not primarily with the economic consequences of this adjustment process but rather with the reduced freedom of action and influence for the United States in

---

[9] This estimate reflects simply the change in cost from oil imports as a fraction of economic output. The current annual GDP is about $13.2 trillion (data from second quarter 2006).

Table 2: Top World Oil Producers, 2004★

	Country	Total Oil Production★★ (million barrels per day)
1)	Saudi Arabia	10.37
2)	Russia	9.27
3)	United States	8.69
4)	Iran	4.09
5)	Mexico	3.83
6)	China	3.62
7)	Norway	3.18
8)	Canada	3.14
9)	Venezuela	2.86
10)	United Arab Emirates	2.76
11)	Kuwait	2.51
12)	Nigeria	2.51
13)	United Kingdom	2.08
14)	Iraq	2.03

★*Table includes all countries' total oil production exceeding 2 million barrels per day in 2004.*

★★*Total oil production includes crude oil, natural gas liquids, condensate, refinery gain, and other liquids.*

Source: See www.eia.doe.gov/emeu/cabs/topworldtables1_2.html.

the conduct of its foreign affairs. In addition to constraining U.S. action, the revenues and dependencies in the world oil market empower oil-rich countries—such as Iran and Venezuela—to carry out foreign policies that are hostile to that of the United States.

Even at today's high prices, global demand is still expected to grow. Prospectively, developed economies are anticipated to increase their consumption of oil at perhaps 1 percent per year, while developing economies such as China, India, Brazil, Indonesia, and Mexico are

---

A $25 per barrel rise in oil prices would increase the annual cost of oil imports (12.7 million barrels per day) by $116 billion, or about 0.9 percent of GDP.

expected to increase their consumption in the range of 3 to 4 percent annually.

Though there will be ups and downs over time, the real price of oil will probably continue to increase. The reason is that for the past one hundred years or so, the United States and other industrialized countries have consumed large amounts of oil, depleting the most readily available "conventional" oil resources. As these low-cost conventional oils are depleted, exploration and production will turn to progressively more expensive sources, such as oil in extremely deep water and tar sands.

So while the world will not soon "run out of oil," these new supplies are almost surely going to be more difficult and expensive to produce than in the past. Production from existing fields is declining, on average, about 5 percent per year (roughly 4.3 million barrels per day), and thus even sustaining current levels of consumption requires an enormous effort. Technology will offer better exploration tools and more efficient techniques for recovery of oil-in-place, but at additional cost. Because the oil price is determined by the cost of the marginal barrel, it is thus more costly oil that will determine the increasing price trajectory in the future.

Myth #4: There's plenty of low-cost oil ready to be tapped.

Unlikely. For the past 150 years the world has used low-cost oil, such as in Saudi Arabia and East Texas. Over the long run, progressively higher-cost sources of oil will need to be tapped. That, on average, will translate into higher oil prices. The world cannot "drill its way out of this problem."

The depletion of conventional sources, especially those close to the major markets in the United States, Western Europe, and Asia, means that the production and transport of oil will become even more dependent on an infrastructure that is already vulnerable. In particular, oil supply is expected to continue to concentrate in the Persian Gulf, which holds the world's largest geologically attractive reserves (table 1), and is a region that has been unstable and includes countries that have periodically used their oil exports for political purposes unfriendly to the United States.

A large fraction of the world's traded oil already passes through a handful of strategic choke points, such as the Strait of Hormuz. The infrastructure for delivering oil has several potential weak links, including major oil processing facilities that are vital yet vulnerable to attack and difficult to repair. In February 2006, terrorists linked to al-Qaeda attempted, but failed, to destroy the Abqaiq processing facility in Saudi Arabia, where 6.8 million barrels per day of oil (some two-thirds of total Saudi production) are processed before export.[10] There have been numerous efforts to strengthen these facilities, both through physical hardening and through improved surveillance and coordination by security services. As the world market for oil relies on increasingly distant sources of supply, often in insecure places, the need to protect the production and transportation infrastructure will grow.

Changes in domestic policies can have significant effects on consumption and production. Such potential effects of policy are particularly pronounced in the United States, which accounts for about one-quarter of the world's oil consumption and one-tenth of oil production. If the United States were to reduce its oil consumption by 10 percent (2.5 percent of world demand), the effect in current tight oil markets could be a temporary decline in global prices (about 12 percent to 25 percent) and a lowering of the anticipated rate of future increases.[11]

In general, policies intended to affect consumption or supply are slow to take effect. Supply projects require long periods of planning, permitting, and construction. Policies intended to affect demand must recognize the large scale of the equipment and facilities that comprise the transportation infrastructure and the long time needed for innovation. For example, in the United States the median age of automobiles is nine years; the full cycle of developing the concept for a new automobile, design, production, and use in the final marketplace extends even longer.

---

[10] The ability of Saudi security services to thwart the Abqaiq attack illustrates that successful protection is possible; a result of the considerable attention the Saudis place on internal security and infrastructure protection.

[11] As in footnote 8, and assuming no immediate changes in supply due to lower prices.

Natural Gas Supply and Demand

The organization of the markets and the role for imports of natural gas are different from that of oil. Until the late 1990s, the North American market for natural gas was essentially independent from other major gas markets. Production of domestic natural gas has not increased sufficiently to meet rising demand and, over the last two decades, the gap has been met mainly by rising imports from Canada. Mexico has not been successful in increasing its production of gas, and Mexico has become a net importer of gas from the United States.

Today, about 2 percent of the total gas supply in North America comes from outside the continent in the form of liquefied natural gas. Most projections envision that LNG will account for a larger share of North American gas supply in the future as demand for gas continues to rise and natural gas production in the United States, Canada, and Mexico is not expected to keep pace (figure 5).

There is well-founded concern about the availability of adequate supplies of natural gas to the North American market over the next several years. Additional gas from less accessible areas of Canada, as well as the long-planned gas pipeline from Alaska to the lower forty-eight states, the Alaskan Natural Gas Transportation System, could augment supply. Most analysts anticipate that LNG will fill the remaining gap. Initially, LNG imports will be a small portion of total North American gas supply but could ultimately prove troublesome in the future if the fraction of LNG in total gas supply rises, creating a dependency on imported gas.

The international natural gas trade will cause a fundamental shift over the coming two decades in the forces that affect gas prices and supplies in the United States. The trade in gas will connect the United States and other major gas-consuming regions of the world through an international gas market. In Europe, the question of security of gas supply already looms large. Russia accounts for about one-quarter of European supplies, while Algeria provides 11 percent, and there are questions about the reliability of these two suppliers. The reliability of the Russian supply has become particularly worrisome after the recent pricing disputes between the Russian giant Gazprom and Belarus and Ukraine, which resulted in brief interruptions of Russian supplies. At

Figure 5: North American Natural Gas Consumption and Production, 1980–2025

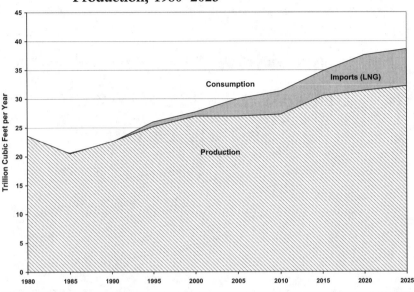

Source: EIA, *Annual Energy Outlook 2005.*

the same time, Gazprom has also threatened additional curtailments if European buyers seek to diversify away from Russian gas. As Europe becomes even more dependent on Russian gas supply, it is likely that European governments will become even more reluctant to challenge Russia's behavior on a wide range of issues, such as nonproliferation and anticorruption. Managing these relationships is first and foremost a task for European policymakers, but there are consequences for the United States as natural gas markets become interconnected.

Over time, there will be growing pressure on the United States to develop the capacity to manage disruptions to gas supplies. The best protection against those insecurities is to sustain the North American natural gas production base. But it is also necessary to integrate the North American natural gas market into an orderly international market for natural gas through a robust network of LNG re-gasification terminals, pipeline transportation, and storage. The market, on its own, is moving in this direction but constructive policy measures, for example, to facilitate siting of LNG facilities and pipelines, are needed.

Findings: How Dependence on Imported Energy Affects U.S. Foreign Policy

The Task Force has identified five major reasons why dependence on energy traded in world markets is a matter of concern for U.S. foreign policy. We have also examined a sixth, the relationship of military force structure to oil dependence.

First, the control over enormous oil revenues gives exporting countries the flexibility to adopt policies that oppose U.S. interests and values. Iran proceeds with a program that appears to be headed toward acquiring a nuclear weapons capability. Russia is able to ignore Western attitudes as it has moved to authoritarian policies in part because huge revenues from oil and gas exports are available to finance that style of government. Venezuela has the resources from its oil exports to invite realignment in Latin American political relationships and to fund changes such as Argentina's exit from its International Monetary Fund (IMF) standby agreement and Bolivia's recent decision to nationalize its oil and gas resources. Because of their oil wealth, these and other producer countries are free to ignore U.S. policies and to pursue interests inimical to our national security.

Second, oil dependence causes political realignments that constrain the ability of the United States to form partnerships to achieve common objectives. Perhaps the most pervasive effect arises as countries dependent on imports subtly modify their policies to be more congenial to suppliers. For example, China is aligning its relationships in the Middle East (e.g., Iran and Saudi Arabia) and Africa (e.g., Nigeria and Sudan) because of its desire to secure oil supplies. France and Germany, and with them much of the European Union, are more reluctant to confront difficult issues with Russia and Iran because of their dependence on imported oil and gas as well as the desire to pursue business opportunities in those countries.

These new realignments have further diminished U.S. leverage, particularly in the Middle East and Central Asia. For example, Chinese interest in securing oil and gas supplies challenges U.S. influence in central Asia, notably in Kazakhstan. And Russia's influence is likely to grow as it exports oil and (within perhaps a decade) large amounts of natural gas to Japan and China.

All consuming countries, including the United States, are more constrained in dealing with producing states when oil markets are tight. To cite one current example, concern about losing Iran's 2.5 million barrels per day of world oil exports will cause importing states to be reluctant to take action against Iran's nuclear program.

Third, high prices and seemingly scarce supplies create fears—especially evident in Beijing and New Delhi, as well as in European capitals and in Washington—that the current system of open markets is unable to ensure secure supply. The present competition has resulted in oil and gas deals that include political arrangements in addition to commercial terms. Highly publicized Chinese oil investments in Africa have included funding for infrastructure projects such as an airport, a railroad, and a telecommunications system, in addition to the agreement that the oil be shipped to China. Many more of these investments also include equity stakes for state-controlled Chinese companies. Another example is Chinese firms taking a position in Saudi Arabia, along with several Western firms, in developing Saudi Arabia's gas infrastructure. At present, these arrangements have little effect on world oil and gas markets because the volumes affected are small. However, such arrangements are spreading. These arrangements are worrisome because they lead to special political relationships that pose difficulties for the United States. And they allow importers to believe that they obtain security through links to particular suppliers rather than from the proper functioning of a global market.

We note that the United States, in the past, has also taken decisions to restrict markets partly due to similar concerns about energy security. For example, when the trans–Alaska pipeline opened, it included a prohibition against exporting the oil. The hostility toward proposals by the Chinese National Overseas Oil Company (CNOOC) to purchase Union Oil of California is seen by some as denying investment opportunity in the U.S. market in a similar manner to what the United States decries about other nations' conduct. The Task Force believes that foreign entities should be able to purchase U.S. assets provided that the acquisitions meet the criteria established by the Committee on Foreign Investment in the United States (CFIUS).[12]

Opening a dialogue with rapidly growing consumers, notably China and India, can help those consumers gain confidence that will lead to a greater willingness to allow markets to operate. (We return to this policy recommendation later.) The United States and other consuming countries have a tremendous interest in maintaining the present open market oil commodity trading rules.

Fourth, revenues from oil and gas exports can undermine local governance. The United States has an interest in promoting good governance both for its own sake and because it encourages investment that can increase the level and security of supply. States that are politically unstable and poorly governed often struggle with the task of responsibly managing the large revenues that come from their oil and gas exports. The elements of good governance include democratic accountability, low corruption, and fiscal transparency. Production in fragile democracies, such as in Nigeria, can be undermined when politicians or local warlords focus on ways to seize oil and gas rents rather than on the longer-term task of governance. Totalitarian governments that have control over those revenue flows can entrench their rule.

When markets are tight, large oil consumers have tended to become especially focused on securing supply and ignore the effects of their investments on corruption and mismanagement. In Sudan, for example, despite civil war and widespread human rights abuses, the Chinese government and its oil enterprises are funding extensive oil supply and

---

[12] Alan P. Larson and David M. Marchick, *Foreign Investment and National Security: Getting the Balance Right, a Council Special Report* (New York: Council on Foreign Relations Press, 2006).

infrastructure projects. China has used its threat of a veto in the UN Security Council to thwart collective efforts by other countries to manage the Darfur crisis in Sudan. Similarly, China, India, and several Western European countries continue to invest in Iran despite the need to contain its nuclear aspirations.

Fifth, a significant interruption in oil supply will have adverse political and economic consequences in the United States and in other importing countries. When such a disruption occurs, it upends all ongoing policy activity in a frantic effort to return to normal conditions. Inevitably, those efforts include matters of foreign policy, such as coordination with other countries to find measures that will mitigate the consequences of the supply disruption. Some of these responses may be preplanned, such as the coordinated release of strategic reserves, but other responses will be hurried, ineffectual, or even counterproductive.

Sixth, some observers see a direct relationship between the dependence of the United States on oil, especially from the Persian Gulf, and the size of the U.S. defense budget. Such a relationship invites the inference that if it were not dependent on this oil, the United States and its allies would have no interest in the region, and hence it would be possible to achieve significant reductions in the U.S. military posture. In the extreme, this argument says that if the nation reduced its dependence, then the defense budget could be reduced as well.

U.S. strategic interests in reliable oil supplies from the Persian Gulf are not proportional with the percent of oil consumption that is imported by the United States from the region. Until very low levels of dependence are reached, the United States and all other consumers of oil will depend on the Persian Gulf. Such low levels will certainly not be reached during the twenty-year time frame of this study.

Even if the Persian Gulf did not have the bulk of the world's readily available oil reserves, there would be reasons to maintain a substantial military capability in the region. The activities of Iran today and Iraq, especially prior to 1991, underline the seriousness of threats from weapons of mass destruction. Combating terrorism also requires a presence in the Gulf. In addition to military activities, a U.S. presence in the region can help to improve political stability.

At least for the next two decades, the Persian Gulf will be vital to U.S. interests in reliable oil supply, nonproliferation, combating terrorism, and encouraging political stability, democracy, and public welfare. Accordingly, the United States should expect and support a strong military posture that permits suitably rapid deployment to the region, if required.

It is worthwhile to explain what should and should not be expected from this military force, and how it serves U.S. interests. Most importantly, the conventional force of the United States deters aggression in the region. Any nation (or subnational group) that contemplates violence on any scale must take into account the possibility of U.S. preemption, intervention, or retaliation. Deterrence is powerful, but it does not always work (especially if the possibility of a military response is not raised). For example, deterrence did not prevent the Iran-Iraq war of the early 1980s. Because no clear and credible signal was sent of a possible response in 1990, Saddam Hussein was not deterred from invading Kuwait. Nevertheless, the U.S. military posture with its capacity to intervene, if managed wisely, can play a role in stabilizing this highly fragile region and make many countries in the region more secure from hostile action by their neighbors.

Several standard operations of U.S. regionally deployed forces have made important contributions to improving energy security, and the continuation of such efforts will be necessary in the future. U.S. naval protection of the sea-lanes that transport oil is of paramount importance. Joint training and exercises with local military units and military-to-military exchanges and support programs also make an important contribution—such as in West Africa, where U.S. naval and Coast Guard units have assisted local authorities in suppressing piracy of crude oil.

Findings and Recommendations: U.S. Domestic Energy Policy

Objectives for Domestic Policy

The need to reduce imports of oil in the United States and to better balance the world oil market leads naturally to the following five policy objectives:

- Increase efficiency of oil and gas use;
- Switch from oil-derived products to alternatives;
- Encourage supply of oil from sources outside the Persian Gulf;
- Make the oil and gas infrastructure more efficient and secure; and
- Increase investment in new energy technologies.

It is important to recognize that in most cases, change will be slow. The enormous magnitude of equipment and facilities that comprise the energy supply and demand system implies that even once technologies begin to be adopted, full replacement of the existing facilities will take several decades.

Increase Efficiency of Oil and Gas Use

The United States needs to adopt technologies and processes that require less energy use for the energy services it receives. Consumers and businesses want energy services, such as transportation, lighting, and air-conditioning. There are combinations of energy, materials, labor, and equipment that can be used to produce most of these energy services more efficiently. For example, a hybrid-electric vehicle provides transportation services that are similar to conventional cars but with different equipment that allows for much more efficient use of gasoline.

When consumers and businesses have sufficient information, they can be expected to choose the technologies and processes that provide the desired energy services at the lowest cost from their perspective. However, the lowest cost option from the perspective of energy users may not be the lowest cost option from the perspective of the United States when broader considerations such as energy security, environmental externalities, and long-term welfare are included. Thus, the United States should adopt policies that encourage consumers and businesses to use less oil and other forms of energy while still obtaining the energy services they need.

Switch from Oil-derived Products to Alternatives

While recognizing that there will be no significant early relief, the United States needs to begin now to adopt technologies and processes that allow for the use of fuels other than those based on petroleum, in particular those alternative fuels that reduce the negative consequences that come from the country's reliance on imported petroleum. For example, oil is still used for space heating of buildings in some regions; however, those buildings could be heated by natural gas directly or, for larger buildings, by efficient cogeneration of electricity and space heating. Cars and other light vehicles could be fueled with increasingly larger fractions of biomass-derived liquids (such as ethanol), and vehicles can be fueled by compressed natural gas. Light duty vehicles could be powered increasingly over time by electricity rather than gasoline or diesel fuel. The current generation of hybrid-electric vehicles may be supplanted by "plug-in hybrids," which allow some fraction of the mileage to be powered by electricity that is charged from the grid, perhaps leading to an eventual transition to fully electric vehicles.[13]

---

[13] These hybrids are powered entirely by gasoline or diesel. Electricity is generated by an onboard internal combustion gasoline (or diesel) engine and is also captured through regenerative braking.

Electric cars and plug-in hybrids require attention to the sources of electricity. Conventional coal-fired electricity (which accounts for the majority of the U.S. power supply) emits CO_2. Advanced coal technologies that make it possible to capture and sequester most of the CO_2 underground are still in their infancy. Some forms of renewable energy, for example, wind, which emits no CO_2, may play an increasing role in the electric grid. At this time, however, most renewable energy projects are not commercially viable without subsidies or regulatory mandates. If the new incremental electric power–generating capacity required for vehicles is fired with natural gas, then electrification could merely shift dependence on imported oil to dependence on imported gas. If the electricity generation is by nuclear power, then a transition to electric and plug-in cars displaces oil. Thus, nuclear power, among other electric power supply options, offers an important long-term pathway to displacing oil as a transportation fuel.

The United States should increase the supply of energy sources that can be used in place of oil in end uses or in electric generation. If natural gas prices are attractive, operators of dual-fired electric generation plants will use natural gas in place of oil. An increase in natural gas supply need not come from conventional sources and might include supply from LNG or unconventional sources, such as coal bed methane and tight sands.

Myth #5: *Renewable energy and nuclear power can quickly reduce dependence on oil and gas.*

Cellulosic biomass, a renewable fuel with a potential for significant scale, is a leading contender to directly displace transportation fuels. However, the full potential of this technology will take time to develop, and there are no commercially viable cellulosic biomass production units in operation today. Moreover, this biomass source of liquid fuels will need to compete with liquid fuels derived from coal and natural gas, which are also attracting investment. Electricity—whether derived from renewable energy (e.g., photovoltaics, hydropower, geothermal, and wind), nuclear, or other sources such as coal— at present substitutes only for a tiny fraction of oil used in the United States and other advanced countries. Improvements in plug-in hybrid and all-electric cars could change that situation in the future.

Biomass offers an important potential source for liquid fuels. At present, significant federal and state subsidies are accelerating the use of ethanol derived from corn and (to a much lesser degree) sugar. New technologies that use cellulosic feedstock to produce biofuels hold the promise of becoming commercially viable while requiring less oil and natural gas per gallon to produce ethanol than today's corn-based technologies, thus replacing significant quantities of oil.

Encourage Supply of Oil from Sources Outside the Persian Gulf

Increases in oil supply can have the same effect on the world oil price as a decline in oil demand. Therefore, the world should be encouraging oil production everywhere. Increased oil supply from sources outside the Persian Gulf, where much oil export is already concentrated, is especially valuable to the world market because it can reduce dependence on this politically fragile region.

Increased supply of oil from U.S. sources, just as increased supply from any source, places a downward pressure on oil prices. But increased supply from U.S. sources has the additional foreign policy benefit of directly reducing imports of oil into the United States.

The supply increases need not be from conventional oil sources. Drawing from the substantial U.S. reserves of unconventional oil and gas—such as tar sands and oil shale—could have the same impacts on world oil price and on U.S. oil imports.[14] Similarly, Canadian development of its unconventional sources, particularly tar sands, could help limit world oil price increases.

Make the Oil and Gas Infrastructure More Efficient and Secure

The infrastructure for the reliable supply of oil and gas can be made more efficient and secure through attention in three areas.

First, oil stockpiles remain essential to protect markets against severe disruptions in supply. The United States and many other oil-importing countries created strategic petroleum reserves in the 1970s to help

---

[14] Although increasing these unconventional sources would have the same foreign policy benefits to the United States, such an increase would cause environmental concerns. New developments in shale oil technology make this source more economic than in the past while also ameliorating some of the past environmental concerns.

manage risks associated with oil supply disruptions. The U.S. reserve now includes almost 700 million barrels of crude oil; the Energy Policy Act of 2005 directs that this be expanded to 1 billion barrels. Oil can be drawn from the reserve in response to a temporary oil market supply disruption and thereby keep world oil prices from rising precipitously. Although originally envisioned to protect against oil supply disruptions from oil-exporting nations, the reserve has been drawn upon to limit crude oil price increases after hurricanes Katrina and Rita reduced U.S. offshore production. While these stocks play an important role, since the 1970s there have been many changes in the context for these reserves. In particular, there is a robust futures market today for oil commodities, and the management of petroleum inventories controlled by private firms has become more sophisticated, which creates a need to reassess the purpose and operation of these reserves.

Second, the U.S. oil and natural gas infrastructure could be made less vulnerable to disruption either from natural disasters or terrorist attacks. Refineries, oil and gas pipelines, and production facilities face such risks. And as was seen after Katrina and Rita, the vulnerability can be indirect: refineries and pipelines were shut down, in part because electricity was not available to power these facilities.

Third, the strategy has been, and should continue to be, improved economic management after oil price jumps. In the 1973–74 crisis, the federal government imposed price and allocation controls on refined petroleum products. Similarly, price controls limited retail price increases when oil prices jumped after the Iranian hostage crisis. These price controls contributed to gasoline shortages that were evident, for example, in long lines at retail gasoline stations. During the more recent spike in prices, the government did not attempt to control supply, and prices were allowed to increase and the market for fuel was allowed to clear, with no lines at gasoline stations. Although high prices are painful for consumers of gasoline and other refined products, shortages created by government intervention can cause even more difficulties.

Increase Investment in New Energy Technologies

Achieving the above four objectives will require the development and deployment of new technologies at commercial scale. The high price of oil is a strong incentive to the private sector to make the investments needed to develop and deploy new technologies. This innovative activity will range from entrepreneurial start-up companies to venture capital funds to large energy and chemical companies. The targets for innovation will include both demand and supply technologies and all fuels from renewables to oil. Just in the past two years, hundreds of start-up companies have been founded in areas from biofuels to batteries. In addition, large oil and chemical companies have launched development projects on biomass, shale, and coal-to-liquids. Research activity has increased dramatically in the nation's universities and laboratories.

These private investments are likely to yield some fruit on their own. However, the pace of the private sector progress depends on a complementary program of federal energy technology research, development, and demonstration projects. The reason is that investment in new energy technologies is made by private sector firms in response to their assessment of future market conditions, which include the expected price of oil, environmental regulations, and government incentives such as tax credits or attractive financing. But, for a variety of reasons, private firms do not take into account the full range of national benefits that come from investment in energy technology R&D.[15] Private investment will fall short of what is needed, and there is a role for government support of R&D toward the other broad goals for domestic energy policy (increasing energy efficiency, facilitating switching away from oil, increasing the supply of oil from both foreign and domestic sources, and allowing for a more secure and capable energy infrastructure).

The Department of Energy (DOE) has responsibility for most of the federal RD&D effort but other agencies also sponsor and perform relevant work. The appropriate mix of RD&D by government agencies, universities, research labs, and private corporations can be debated, as can the proper mix of research, development, and demonstration

---

[15] Among the many reasons why private firms do not invest in R&D at a level commensurate with the large benefits that R&D offers to society: intellectual property rights are incomplete, particularly for long-term R&D; energy technology advances often have important spillovers to other technologies that might not benefit the firms doing the R&D; and, absent credible policy commitments and economic incentives, firms cannot expect to capture the national security and environmental benefits of their new technology investments.

projects. However, the Task Force is critical of the continuing U.S. federal RD&D effort; it is fragmented, unfocused, and tries to be all things to all people. More investment in new energy technologies on the supply and demand side of energy markets is needed as part of a long-term energy policy strategy if the United States is to adequately manage the transition away from a petroleum-based economy.

Task Force Recommendations to Achieve Domestic Policy Objectives

Task Force members believe that there are many domestic policy instruments that could be used to achieve the five objectives.

Increase Energy Efficiency

The Task Force is unanimous in concluding that stronger incentives are needed to encourage investment in energy efficiency and fuel switching by the hundreds of millions of consumers and commercial enterprises in the United States. Individual users must face prices for energy services that are brought in line with the full costs incurred by the United States from importing oil.

Because two-thirds of the oil used in the U.S. economy is for transportation, and most of that (60 percent) is used in personal vehicles such as automobiles, minivans, and sport-utility vehicles (SUVs), special attention is needed for policy instruments that could slow the growth in demand for gasoline.

One measure would reduce the growth in demand for gasoline over time: a substantial federal excise tax on gasoline.[16] Such a tax would

---

[16] As an example, consider a gasoline tax of $1 per gallon added to a gasoline price that would otherwise be $3 per gallon. We assume that the entire $1 would become part of the gasoline price so that the gasoline price would become $4 per gallon. Over the first several years, such a tax could be expected to reduce the use of gasoline by between 3 percent and 6 percent from its otherwise expected growth path. Most of this response would result from people driving less, although some would result from multiple-car families using the more fuel-efficient of the vehicles available. Over a course of ten or more years, the largest impact could be the fuel economy of the vehicles purchased. If one assumed a demand elasticity of 0.6, such a gasoline tax could reduce long-run use of gasoline by about 16 percent from its otherwise expected growth path. A $1 per gallon gasoline tax would still leave gasoline prices lower than those typical in the European nations.

encourage less driving as well as increased efforts by automakers to develop and market more fuel-efficient vehicles. The impacts on oil imports would be small at first but would grow over time as the total fleet of vehicles became more efficient. However, over the years, this measure has faced insurmountable opposition.

A second measure would tighten and reform the Corporate Average Fuel Economy rules. These rules, enacted in 1975 in the wake of the first oil crisis, set minimum average fuel economies (miles per gallon) on the domestically produced and imported fleets of new vehicles sold by each manufacturer each year.[17] An advantage of reforming and tightening CAFE standards is that such changes would lead to greater fuel economy than expected from likely increases in gasoline prices.[18] A disadvantage is that CAFE focuses on the fuel economy of vehicles and provides no incentives for reduced driving. If increased CAFE standards would make driving less costly by forcing more efficient cars on the road, people would offset some of the benefits by driving more.

The third option would be to place a cap on gasoline consumption and adopt a system of tradable vouchers. This approach would have a similar incentive effect as a tax, but would redistribute income among consumers. Consumers in rural or suburban areas, who drive more than average, could purchase vouchers from consumers in urban areas who drive less than average. With a gasoline tax, the amount of the tax would be known but the actual consumption of gasoline would be somewhat uncertain, depending on weather, consumer tastes, season of year, and consumer response to higher prices. With vouchers, the consumption would be fixed but the price of the vouchers could fluctuate sharply in response to the same factors. Changes in consumer beliefs about future gasoline demand changes could lead to radical and

---

[17] The averaging was more precisely of gallons per mile for each make and model, weighted by the number of vehicles sold of the various makes and models. That average is different from averaging miles per gallon, using the same weights.

[18] As an example, a 40 percent increase in the CAFE standards would reduce gasoline use by 29 percent once the fleet of vehicles completely turned over, if there were no impacts on driving. However, if this gasoline reduction also reduced the fuel cost per mile of driving by 20 percent, total driving could be expected to increase by between 3.5 percent and 7 percent, leading to a net reduction in gasoline use of between 24 percent and 26 percent.

rapid shifts in the market prices of the vouchers.[19] The Task Force does not agree on which measures, used singly or in combination, would be best.

Numerous other policies could have an effect on fuel consumption as well. Many experts note that a shift from cars to mass transit could have a major effect in reducing oil consumption, in addition to other benefits. Where such actions substitute electricity for oil, such as in subways and other electrified trains, these policies may enhance energy security as well. However, expanding electricity-generating capacity and electricity transmission in the United States is not without its challenges.

Other mechanisms have also been proposed and/or implemented for increasing energy efficiency outside of the transportation sectors and for increasing the amount of fuel switching away from oil.[20]

Switch from Oil-derived Products to Alternatives

In order to substitute alternatives for oil, those substitutes must be available at a cost that consumers see as competitive with oil. Many different policy instruments can be used, and some have been adopted to increase the availability of oil alternatives while reducing their cost to consumers.

The protectionist $0.54 per gallon tariff on imported ethanol should be removed. Such an action would make it easier for domestic fuel suppliers to introduce more biomass-derived liquid fuels into the U.S. market from countries such as Brazil, where ethanol production is much more cost-effective than in the United States. While an important step, elimination of the tariff is likely to have only a relatively small positive impact on supply initially because the countries with major

---

[19] For example, if expected near-term demand for gasoline increased 5 percent, the price of vouchers would increase by between 25 percent and 50 percent of the gasoline price plus voucher price, say between $1 and $2 per gallon voucher price increase.

[20] Examples include: weatherization programs for residential buildings; utility-based energy efficiency investments; Energy Star designations for appliances; building standards and heating, ventilating, and air conditioning (HVAC) standards for buildings; "flex your power" alerts encouraging reduction in electricity use on peak power days; and rebate programs for reducing electricity usage below levels measured for the previous year. Suggestions include: mandates requiring flexible-fuel vehicles; fuel tax exemptions for alternative fuels; and renewable portfolio standards for blending of liquids with gasoline.

export potential based on current ethanol technology have, at present, only limited production capacity. Newer ethanol technologies offer greater promise and will be considered below.

The Task Force believes that the United States should make greater use of nuclear power. With high natural gas prices and concern about CO_2 emissions, there is renewed interest in nuclear power. In the near term, new nuclear plants will be ordered and built only if the U.S. government is successful in making clear progress on nuclear waste management, creating a reasonable regulatory framework for licensing nuclear plants with acceptable safety risk, and meeting proliferation concerns. In turn, the additional electricity supply will eventually make it easier to achieve greater substitution of electricity for oil, such as through use of plug-in hybrid cars and other cost-effective electricity-based transportation technologies.

Encourage Supply of Oil from All Sources

While oil output from the United States is declining and gas production is flat, some potentially rich fields have remained off limits. These include the Arctic National Wildlife Refuge (ANWR) in Alaska, off-shore southern California, the east coast of Florida, the Gulf of Mexico, and publicly controlled areas in the Rocky Mountains. Opening of some of these areas could reduce the rate of decline of U.S. production.

However, drilling in all these areas—especially ANWR and off the coasts of California and Florida—has been very controversial. Environmental groups have strongly objected to drilling in ANWR; the states of California and Florida have strongly objected to drilling off their coasts.

The United States also holds substantial reserves of unconventional oil and gas, such as tar sands, oil shale, and deep gas. These deposits have historically been costly to extract, but higher hydrocarbon prices along with improved technologies make them more feasible today. Most of the U.S. tar sands resource, which totals about 20 billion barrels, is found in eastern Utah, located mainly on public lands. However, the Task Force notes that there are formidable environmental obstacles, including the large amounts of energy (and thus CO_2 emissions) required to extract and process these heavy oils.

Taken together, the potential increase in domestic conventional oil production would make only a modest contribution to total U.S. supply. However, one of the foreign policy energy security goals of the United States is to encourage other countries to make investments in maintaining or increasing their production. Visible steps to increase oil production in the United States could play an important role in convincing other countries to expand their production.

Make the U.S. Energy Infrastructure More Efficient and Secure

A well-functioning and efficient energy infrastructure should keep the cost of distribution of energy from producers to consumers as low as possible while also assuring that the energy system is able to adjust reliably to perturbations. The United States should take several measures to strengthen its energy infrastructure to achieve these two goals.

First, the U.S. energy infrastructure must be made less vulnerable to disruption from natural disasters and terrorist attacks. Despite many warnings and much talk, efforts to bring the government and industry together to make the oil, gas, and electricity infrastructure less vulnerable have delivered mixed results. On the one hand, federal and some state regulators, working with industry, have taken steps to reduce vulnerabilities. These include a recent program, led by industry and endorsed by the Federal Energy Regulatory Commission (FERC), to encourage utilities to build and share stockpiles of spare transformers. On the other hand, the robustness of the oil, gas, and electricity infrastructures remain unknown in important ways; hurricanes Katrina and Rita served as a reminder that much additional effort remains. Reducing the vulnerability and improving the robustness of other energy infrastructure facilities, for example, power plants and the electric grid, are important. The U.S. government must develop a policy, beyond the present ad hoc arrangements, to clarify who should pay for these improvements.

Second, the U.S. refinery industry is beset by many regulations that are reducing the incentive for needed investment to upgrade the capacity to process larger amounts of heavier crude oils. Consider these examples: the local requirement to refine fuels with much lower sulfur content to reduce harmful particulate emissions, the undisciplined proliferation of highly specialized and distinct fuel formulas—"boutique fuels"—that impede the efficient operation of the fuel infrastructure, possible limitation on aromatics, and the shifting motivation about adding oxygenates such as MTBE and ethanol to reformulated gasoline.[21] The cost and benefit of these regulations should be reviewed given their cumulative effect on the refinery industry.

Third, the United States should review its policy and program for the strategic petroleum reserve (SPR). The SPR, established in the late 1970s, is an important tool for moderating the effects of politically motivated interruptions and signaling the market about supply availability. However, the oil market has changed considerably in recent years—in particular, there has been a rise of futures trading that allows market-based hedging of risks—and it is advisable to consider the implications of such changes in the oil market for the structure and operation of the SPR. What is the appropriate SPR security objective in light of today's global marketplace realities, which are dramatically different from the 1970s? Does the expected rise in market share of OPEC in future decades influence the answer? Should the purpose of the SPR and other national reserves be strictly to ameliorate the effect of massive disruptions or should they also be employed to ameliorate price volatility due to real or anticipated modest disruptions associated with political or weather events or accidents that temporarily disrupt supply?

Revising this statement of objectives would provide the guidance needed for a sensible reexamination of SPR authorities and related questions. Should the size of the SPR be increased, perhaps expanding the storage of processed petroleum products (as opposed to crude oil, which is the commodity stored currently in the SPR)? Does the emergence of petroleum and natural gas futures markets influence the need for the SPR? How should the rules for allocation from the SPR be changed?[22] For example, how useful is an oil swap between the SPR and an oil supplier as a market signal in a momentarily tight

---

[21] MTBE (methyltertiarybutylethane) was originally proposed as an additive to motor gasoline in the 1970s to replace lead as an octane enhancer.

[22] The DOE, in response to the 2005 Energy Policy Act, currently is proposing change to the SPR allocation procedures.

market and as a way of adding oil to the SPR? Will effectiveness be compromised or enhanced with more frequent use of swaps or similar arrangements? DOE has the authority to enter into "swaps" for SPR oil—to accept a greater amount of oil in the future as a charge for release of oil to a private entity today. Although oil companies are skeptical about DOE's involvement in the market, swaps have the merits of exercising the SPR machinery and adding oil without congressional appropriations, and the effect is to dampen price volatility without affecting time-averaged prices.

The European Union (EU) has no comparable swap authority because of the way the EU runs its system of reserves. This underlines the need for international reexamination of how reserves are best structured and used in light of today's global marketplace realities.

Fourth, it is especially important that the United States takes steps to facilitate the introduction of LNG and other forms of natural gas from abroad into North America. The Federal Energy Regulatory Commission has recently established procedures for the rapid consideration and approval of LNG re-gasification facilities and new natural gas pipelines that improve the connectivity of the United States, Mexico, and Canada. However, local opposition to these projects has created delays and in some cases killed the projects. Opposition is especially strong in areas of the United States that are also remote from gas supplies and could benefit from a larger role for LNG, such as in the Northeast and in the far West.

Increase Investment in New Energy Technologies

Investments in new energy technologies are made by private sector firms in response to their assessment of future economic conditions and changing market and government incentives. In addition, the federal government, mostly through DOE, directly supports a wide range of new energy technology activities.

Although the R&D undertaken by both the public and private sector is intrinsically risky, examination of DOE energy R&D projects has shown that even though most projects yielded few (or no) public benefits, the ones that were successful provided national benefits significantly exceeding the total cost of the energy R&D program.[23] The same pattern is typical of private sector research or investment by venture capital firms. This pattern implies the need for a portfolio of technology programs, aiming at different technological goals, with different time horizons.

The role of the government in funding energy research and some types of development is generally accepted. The Task Force supports the importance of governmental research, development, and demonstration supporting a wide range of technology investments on the supply and demand sides of energy markets.

In addition to RD&D that is funded and performed by government, the public sector also has a role in providing incentives for private sector new energy technology development. Congress has periodically adopted tax credits for broad-based R&D or for energy-specific R&D. Such credits encourage the private sector to multiply the effect of governmental efforts. The Task Force supports such governmental incentives for private sector research and development.

Once R&D has been conducted, demonstration projects may be necessary. However, the costs of demonstration projects are many times higher than the R&D costs. There are instances of successful demonstration projects and many instances of highly expensive failures. In some cases, demonstration projects are essential for engineering first-of-a-kind plants and for showing whether such plants can be built and operated in a manner that meets technical performance specifications, costs, and environmental regulations. Such information can prepare the ground for fuller deployment of new technologies by commercial firms. Some of the technologies that could play a large role in reducing dependence on imported energy are marked by technical risks, high costs, and regulatory uncertainties—these risks can be resolved by well-designed demonstration projects, so that private firms can become more confident that an investment in the technology will be commercially viable. The marketplace on its own will not make the necessary investment. However, the Task Force does not give a blanket endorsement

---

[23] National Research Council, *Energy Research at DOE: Was It Worth It? Energy Efficiency and Fossil Energy Research 1978 to 2000* (Washington, DC: National Academy Press, 2001).

to demonstration projects. The merits of a particular demonstration project, of course, require an assessment of probable benefits, costs, and risks of such demonstrations. The federal government and private companies should cooperatively fund demonstration projects.

A number of particular endeavors appear to have significant potential for government-sponsored technology development:

- Improvement of the mileage of today's automobiles through better vehicle and engine design, including demonstrating compatibility with alternative fuels, such as ethanol.
- Further development of hybrid and electric vehicles, including battery technologies.
- Production of ethanol and other biofuels from cellulosic biomass, e.g., switchgrass.
- Synthetic fuels from coal with carbon capture and sequestration.
- Advanced technologies for hydrocarbon exploration and for enhanced production that recover a greater fraction of the oil-in-place.
- Research on advanced fission technologies and on fusion energy.

The Task Force believes these and other technologies offer important options for reducing U.S. dependence on imported oil. Care is needed, however, in evaluating their costs and benefits, and ultimate potential. New technologies and fuels will need to be evaluated on an economic basis relative to the existing oil system.

The Task Force recommends that the U.S. government substantially increase RD&D spending on alternatives to oil-based fuels and vehicle technologies; it also encourages industry to expand its innovation effort. Finally, we note that there will be opportunities for both the private sector and the U.S. government for new technology development collaboration with international partners—for example, on coal liquefaction accompanied by CO_2 capture and sequestration with government and private research institutes in China.

Success in this venture will require congressional support for private sector investment as well as endorsement of a sensible DOE-managed plan for developing the needed portfolio of new technologies. Congress should support a larger, more comprehensive, and sustained energy RD&D program and avoid prescribing projects and programs that primarily serve special interests. In the past, the DOE RD&D program has been too fragmented and hence was less effective because of excessive congressional attention to projects and technologies that serve local, rather than national, objectives.

Findings and Recommendations: The Conduct of U.S. Foreign Policy

Over many years and administrations, the U.S. government has failed to pay sufficient attention to energy in its conduct of foreign policy or to adopt a consistent approach to energy issues. The result is that energy matters typically appear on the foreign policy agenda as a surprise, usually in times of crisis, or as the unexpected consequence of other foreign policy actions. The foreign policy apparatus resolves energy issues with ad hoc decisions. As a crisis abates, the issues cease to attract attention.

The situation will improve only when energy issues become an integral part of the policymaking process and when these issues receive sustained attention during all stages of policy development and implementation. At the same time, it would be neither practical nor wise to suggest that energy security should be the central foreign policy priority of the United States. U.S. foreign policy, like the foreign policies of most countries, does and must consist of multiple competing priorities. Improving the integration of energy policy and foreign policy, and elevating the importance of energy security in formulating and implementing specific foreign policy objectives, does not offer an escape from the need to make trade-offs among competing objectives on a case-by-case basis. On the contrary, it makes that foreign policy enterprise more complicated and more difficult. While the United States must give sustained attention to energy issues, the nation must not always give priority to matters of energy at the expense of other foreign policy objectives.

In this section, the Task Force suggests a set of five goals, with supporting actions for each, that will improve the nation's ability to manage its dependence on hydrocarbon fuels while pursuing other foreign policy goals at the same time.

Expand Sources of Oil and Gas Production and Protect Transit Routes of these Fuels to Markets

Even with an aggressive effort to control demand for oil and gas, world consumption of these fuels is likely to continue rising in the years ahead. Thus, it is essential to ensure an expanding base for producing and delivering new supplies to world markets.

An important task for U.S. energy security is to seek stability in the Persian Gulf so that this region can sustain and expand reliable production. It will not be easy to balance the desirability of this action with other important foreign policy objectives, for example, with respect to Saudi Arabia, Iran, and Iraq.

- Saudi Arabia—The global market critically depends on expanded production, but at the same time the United States should support steady progress on social reform and a move away from religious fundamentalism that destabilizes governments in the region.

- Iran—U.S. efforts to avoid nuclear proliferation and contain terrorism compete with action to normalize economic relations, which would lead to greater oil output.

- Iraq—Expanded oil production requires improvement in the political and security situation.

Given the challenges in the region that possesses the world's most abundant and least costly hydrocarbon resources, the United States must also continue encouraging production outside of the Persian Gulf. Such growth in production has long been a U.S. policy objective. There are many opportunities to diversify production sources that, taken together, can play a significant role (although they are not as important, in total volume, as the potential and likely role of the Persian Gulf). For example, the U.S. government, working with other governments and firms, has been encouraging production in the Caspian Sea and in Central Asia.

As with production, greater diversity is also welcome in the transportation routes that carry the oil and gas to market. The U.S. government promoted the Baku-Tblisi-Ceyhan pipeline project as part of a policy to create multiple outlets for Central Asian oil, so that not all exports flowed through Russia. Such diversity in transportation routes for oil and gas exports supports effective markets, regardless of the final destination—whether to China, Japan, or other countries.

Higher energy prices have already encouraged private firms to make additional investments in oil production outside the Persian Gulf, such as in Canada's oil sands. In addition to this welcome trend, efforts to encourage production in some areas—notably Russia—will require active policy efforts. Russia is the world's second-largest oil exporter as well as the largest producer and exporter of natural gas, on which Western Europe depends heavily. Russia plays an important role in many other international issues from stability in Central Asia to cooperation with Iran, including on its nuclear program.

In the past three years, Russia has taken steps to place its oil and gas production and transportation system under greater central government control. The implication of this trend is that Russian oil and gas exports will increasingly serve political purposes, probably at the expense of the expansion of Russia's hydrocarbon sector. Russia is a major oil and gas exporter, and the United States has an interest in that country maintaining and expanding production. Thus, despite important differences in foreign policy objectives that divide the United States and Russia, the United States should continue to seek appropriate opportunities for opening the Russian oil sector to foreign investment and facilitating the use of advanced Western technology that will increase Russia's efficiency and level of production.

Encourage Efficiency of Energy Use in All Markets

The United States and other importing countries benefit from additional supplies or reduced demand wherever they occur. Other countries, just as the United States, can make great improvements in efficiency of energy use.

The United States should work with other countries to discourage the practice of subsidizing energy consumption—a practice that has generally declined worldwide over the last two decades but is still widespread. In some countries, including both producing and consuming countries—for example, Indonesia, India, Iran, China, Venezuela, Mexico, and Russia—energy products remain subsidized. Allowing energy prices to rise to world market levels would encourage users to become more efficient in their use of energy and would also encourage additional investment in both energy supply and innovation for greater end-use efficiency. Of course, as market prices rise, government should and will give consideration to targeted assistance programs for the poor and the elderly.

Promote the Proper Functioning and Efficiency of Integrated Energy Markets

Domestic oil and gas markets are part of a global system. It is in the interest of the United States and other consuming and producing nations to facilitate the smooth operation of these markets and eschew, as much as possible, the use of hydrocarbon trade as a political instrument. If markets are open, economic forces will naturally encourage greater efficiency.

U.S. foreign policy should encourage the move to more efficient markets through measures already mentioned, such as encouraging countries to remove subsidies for energy. But there are other actions that the United States can take to improve the operation of energy markets.

First, U.S. foreign policy can encourage a regulatory process that allows the timely construction of cross-border infrastructures that are required for these markets, such as gas pipelines and electric power lines between Canada, Mexico, and the United States. The North American Free Trade Agreement (NAFTA) offers a framework for such investments that, while helpful, is limited. For example, Mexico's domestic opposition to foreign investment in the energy infrastructure is an obstacle to reform, which the United States has had little ability to influence.

Second, accurate historical data and objective projections are needed to inform both private investors and government decision-makers. In the 1970s, data collection and dissemination was one of the important missions assigned to the newly established International Energy Agency. The United States established the Energy Information Administration with the similar purpose of providing transparent and objective data and projections. With the strain on production caused by the rapid increase in demand, the need for accurate worldwide data has once again gained importance. The United States can make a significant contribution by advocating better data collection and analysis of trends for all countries. Such data, if objective, could be influential in bringing reality to decision-makers in both producing and consuming countries.

Third, national oil companies are playing an increasing role in world energy production. The rise in oil prices has strengthened this trend in many countries, in part because higher revenues make NOCs and their parent governments less dependent on foreign investment. The United States must recognize that NOCs are a dominant force in the world oil and gas markets and find ways to work with these enterprises. Indeed, it is impractical for the U.S. government to reverse the trend toward national control. The history of Mexico is relevant in this regard: despite the urging of reform over many years by both Mexican and U.S. officials and energy experts, the constitutional prohibition on foreign ownership of Mexican hydrocarbon reserves appears deeply rooted in Mexico's culture and values. PEMEX and other NOCs should be encouraged to participate in world energy markets in ways that are transparent and conducive to the transfer of technology and capital to expand global production of hydrocarbons.

The United States should encourage NOCs to become more efficient. The tools that are available to the government for this purpose are to encourage private sector investment, joint ventures, and technology transfer. Ultimately, improved performance by NOCs is best accomplished if those firms are exposed to competition in their home markets. Nonetheless, the U.S. government and the business community must accept the fact that NOCs are here to stay and that it is in the U.S.

interest to work with NOCs in a manner that serves a joint interest in improving exploration and production efficiency.

Revitalize International Institutions and Collective International Efforts

U.S. foreign policy should work to build and revitalize international efforts around three tasks:

First, the United States should work with other countries to prepare the world market for oil to better withstand price shocks. In the aftermath of the first oil shock in 1973, the United States and other oil-importing countries created the IEA as a government-to-government mechanism for sharing the pain of oil shocks. World oil markets have changed radically since the IEA was originally created, but the original purpose remains valid: to adopt a common policy concerning government-controlled oil stocks and procedures for sharing shortages should a supply disruption occur. However, changes are needed in both the participants and procedures to accommodate new realities in the world energy markets. Despite the emergence of a robust futures market for oil, a government-controlled petroleum reserve retains both strategic significance (to deter some short-term interruptions) and tactical significance (to signal government policy resolve and direction in a time of political uncertainty created by a disturbance).

To complement a reexamination of the U.S. strategic reserve (addressed in the previous section of this report), a fresh look is needed at the international level. In particular, the United States should encourage the IEA to work with new major energy consumers such as China and India. It may be impractical to expand the IEA formally, as its constitution requires its members to also be part of the Organization for Economic Cooperation and Development (OECD). While the IEA would be the best forum for this effort, a greatly strengthened International Energy Forum could serve this purpose.[24]

---

[24] The International Energy Forum was established in 2003 to promote a ministerial dialogue between major energy producers and consumers. To be usable for the purposes of this Task Force's recommendations, the IEF would need to put substantially greater emphasis on the interests of major energy consumers.

Second, the Task Force notes the large and growing dependence on vulnerable energy infrastructures and a few dangerous straits, such as Hormuz in the Persian Gulf and Malacca in Asia. Critical oil and gas pipelines, such as those in Central Asia, are also vulnerable. Domestically, the United States is struggling to address such infrastructure protection.[25]

U.S. foreign policy can do much to encourage companies and countries to devote greater attention and resources to energy infrastructure protection. Many efforts require coordination between suppliers and users of energy and imply joint action by a coalition of countries that historically have not cooperated. The United States should take the lead in building an infrastructure protection program that would be based on practical steps by relevant countries and address critical infrastructures and transit routes. Initial efforts should focus on joint planning, technical assistance, and military exercises, especially involving naval units operating near ports or along critical sea-lanes.

Third, U.S. foreign policy should do more to promote better management of oil revenues because good management serves the long-term U.S. interest in encouraging increased oil production.

The Task Force has considered the question of whether revenues from the sale of oil, gas, and other minerals undercut good governance—a process often given the emotive term the "resource curse." While the conditions that link resources to poor governance are complex,

---

[25] In the United States, many agencies have responsibility for different aspects of energy infrastructure protection—the problem is an absence of effective coordination. The Department of Energy has some responsibility, as the Sector-Specific Agency, to lead the U.S. effort in identifying energy infrastructure vulnerability assessments and protection requirements. The Department of Defense is involved with critical infrastructure protection, but does not defend specific sites in the United States unless called upon. The Minerals Management Service (MMS) sets, and has recently strengthened, standards for offshore platforms. The Coast Guard also has responsibility for protecting ports, where oil and gas infrastructure is often located. FERC has federal regulatory oversight for interstate pipelines and transmission lines, but state regulators are responsible for local distribution facilities and intrastate lines. Finally, private industries that operate oil and gas facilities have a large stake in keeping them secure, and they are part of the community involved in assessing risks and working with local, state, and federal government agencies to protect them. Given this diffusion of responsibility and authority for protecting the various components of energy infrastructure in the United States, progress has been uneven. Efforts in the United States have been aided by growing attention to infrastructure security following the September 11 terrorist attacks and after hurricanes Katrina and Rita exposed vulnerabilities onshore and offshore in the Gulf of Mexico region.

there are many situations where oil revenues have not improved governance or economic and social conditions. Examples include Nigeria, Chad, and Turkmenistan.

The Task Force recommends that the United States, in conjunction with its allies or international agencies, play a stronger role in pressing for the use of mechanisms that could improve the proper management of hydrocarbon revenues. The Task Force is mindful that it will be difficult to affect the internal decisions of sovereign states, and thus it recommends that these efforts to promote good governance be focused in a few countries where the outcomes would be important—for example, in Nigeria where oil production has the potential to rise significantly but political instability is impeding production and some investment. At this writing, such governance troubles have shut in approximately 500,000 to 700,000 barrels per day of Nigeria's production.

The Task Force notes that it is impractical for the United States to exert much leverage acting alone. The United States imposes strict standards on U.S. firms under the 1977 Foreign Corrupt Practices Act (FCPA). But others, such as European firms and especially Chinese firms, are not similarly constrained. Efforts by the United States to expand FCPA-like rules through the OECD and through the boards of Export Credit Agencies (ECAs) have not been successful. Nor have multilateral efforts proven easy to pursue: the World Bank has struggled to make Chad maintain its commitment to poverty reduction using revenues obtained from oil development and pipeline construction that were funded with a World Bank loan.

The Task Force believes a different approach is needed—one that relies on more extensive (and voluntary) cooperation with host governments. The best example of this approach is the Extractive Industries Transparency Initiative, which is sponsored by the British government, various international financial institutions, and NGOs. EITI's goal is to ensure accountability in the flow of funds to host governments. Accountability, in turn, should make it easier to ensure that funds are spent productively and not siphoned into corruption. EITI's goals are appropriately modest and its instruments are well calibrated to what can be achieved. EITI is off to a promising start in Nigeria and Azerbaijan.[26]

---

[26] An earlier initiative, "Publish What You Pay," which focused on Angola, had little effect on government behavior—firms that adhered to the strictures and published their payments

Figure 6: Trends in Rising Chinese Oil Imports, Prices, and Number of Political Oil Deals

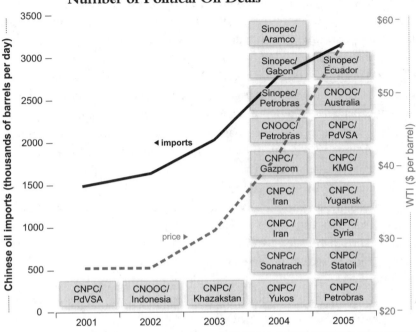

Source: Sinopec Corp., CNOOC Limited, and China National Petroleum Corporation. Price data from *BP Statistical Review of World Energy 2006.* Import data from *EIA China Country Analysis Brief,* August 2006.

The Task Force chose to examine the behavior of Chinese oil companies and the Chinese government as illustrative of market governance problems because of the anticipated growth of Chinese oil imports and because China's activity in world oil markets is in the public eye. Figure 6 presents the accelerating pace of recent oil deals that Chinese state-controlled enterprises have made with major resource holders. Most, but not all, of these deals involve state-to-state arrangements in which China has offered a range of concessions, such as building airports (and, in some cases, indirectly supplying arms), in addition to commercial terms. The rising number of these deals has coincided with higher prices for oil in the world market and China's swelling petroleum imports. There is no simple causal relationship between these factors.

were penalized by the Angolan government. This experience is a reminder that EITI is also unlikely to prove to be effective without indigenous political will.

However, their simultaneous occurrence has raised concerns about whether these arrangements will become even more numerous in the future, with more widespread negative consequences for governance in oil-rich countries and possibly even broader consequences for the world oil market.

Two responses to China's activity to acquire oil resources are equally unsatisfactory. The first is wholly to ignore this Chinese activity on the grounds that the United States has more important foreign policy issues at stake with the Chinese than oil dependence, and that Chinese overspending to "lock up" oil reserves should have no adverse economic effect on world markets. The second response is to assume that the Chinese activity in world energy markets is so potentially disruptive to the underlying political relationships between major resource holder countries and industrialized countries such as the United States that this activity should be seen as another signal of an unavoidable strategic competition between China and the United States.

The Task Force advises against adopting either extreme response. As attention to energy issues rises, the potential for diplomatic conflict with China also rises. Such conflicts could overshadow other important aspects of the U.S.–China relationship. At the same time, these political energy arrangements are leading other countries—notably Korea and India—to adopt similar practices.

The Task Force urges the governments of the United States and China (possibly with other major emerging energy consumers, such as India) to explore areas of common interest. We believe that direct engagement on energy issues of common interest could convince the Chinese of their long-term interest in jointly working to greater world production offered in open energy markets. Through direct engagement, the United States and China will gain a better understanding of the other's approach to matters of energy security; that greater awareness, in turn, will help to reduce tensions.

Integrate Energy Issues into the U.S. Foreign Policy Apparatus

The Task Force is unanimous in the view that energy issues have not received sufficient attention in the formulation and implementation of

U.S. foreign policy. Moreover, the Task Force has stressed that the domestic and foreign policy and security aspects of energy issues cannot be fully disentangled. Thus, there is a need to elevate energy issues in the foreign policy decision-making process across the board and an accompanying need for better integration of the foreign and domestic policy aspects of energy issues. Sustained political attention is required for many reasons—the patterns of energy use and trade, the development of energy technology projects, and the deployment of capital take many years.

Greater awareness of energy issues will make some improvement, but that is not enough. Organizational change is needed. But, it is not clear which specific organizational remedies will accomplish the objective of achieving greater attention and integration of energy issues in the policy process. Ultimately, success depends on the priority that the president and the cabinet place on energy in future administrations.

The Task Force offers a number of measures that if adopted would contribute to a process more likely to give energy issues their required attention.

First, a directorate for energy should be established at the National Security Council—akin to the regional and functional directorates that presently exist on issues such as counterproliferation, defense policy, and international economics. This directorate would lead an interagency working group process that prepares papers to influence the discussion and thinking of the NSC principals, thus leading to better informed and wider options in matters that involve energy and national security. More ambitiously, this new energy directorate could provide support to the NSC, the National Economic Council (NEC), and White House Chief of Staff to help with better integration of domestic and security aspects of energy issues.

Second, the secretary of energy should both be kept fully informed and have a seat at the table in all foreign policy matters that have an important energy aspect. While all matters of foreign policy do not centrally involve energy, it is striking how many now do. Energy issues tend to get shuffled aside because they are not immediate—long-term implications have difficulty competing for policymakers' attention. But energy issues are involved in U.S. relations with Russia, Saudi Arabia,

Nigeria, Venezuela, Canada, Mexico, and other major oil and gas producers. In addition, they include China and also India, which are not only rising consumers of energy but may also become large users of U.S.-origin nuclear power technology—a topic on which the secretary of energy also plays a crucial role. The G8 summit in 2006 focused on energy security; numerous UN gatherings consider the ways that energy contributes to economic growth and affects environmental quality.

Third, high priority should be given to ensure that the terms of reference of all strategic planning studies, in the NSC, State and Defense departments, and intelligence community, require attention to energy security issues and to energy–foreign policy linkages.

The measures that the Task Force recommends, if implemented, would help advance the integration of energy issues into foreign policy deliberations. However, these recommendations alone will not adequately integrate security considerations into the domestic policy process. More is needed to achieve a fully integrated approach to critical trade-offs in energy policy and foreign policy.

The root of the organizational problem lies in the range of considerations that go into a comprehensive energy policy—economic performance; foreign policy; security; environmental impact at local, regional, national, and global scales; balance of foreign trade and investment; industrial competitiveness; fiscal and tax policy; RD&D policy and expenditures; land-use and natural resource management; and others. The secretary of energy does not have the authority to weave together these many threads. They touch upon core interests and responsibilities across the administration. Energy issues also have local and regional impacts that, in turn, attract the interest of members of Congress and congressional committees, as well as state and local government. Within the administration, authority can derive only from the president, who should direct the secretary of energy to lead systematic discussions, with high-level participation from other agencies, in order to produce options for the president's decision. This would also serve to give the administration a clear voice in dealing with Congress on energy matters.

There is no entity within the executive office of the president that is ideal for managing this process. One possibility is to charge the NSC directorate recommended above to perform this function, as long as it is clearly understood that security is but one of the core concerns being blended together with economic, environmental, and other concerns. Another possibility is to establish an interagency group that is not crisis driven, with the Department of Energy and the Department of State playing lead roles in setting the agenda. A third possibility is to establish yet another crosscutting group within the executive office of the president, as was done with the establishment of the Department of Homeland Security, but this approach risks weakening the authority of the responsible agency.

But the conclusion remains: insufficient attention is given to energy, and energy and foreign policy considerations are inadequately integrated in the policymaking process.

While we have focused on actions for organization of the executive branch, the Task Force stresses that improvement in the nation's ability to address matters related to energy security also requires concerted efforts in Congress. Congressional committees with oversight responsibility should reinforce, through hearings and committee actions, a fuller public understanding of the nature and depth of U.S. energy problems and also seek greater integration of energy issues in foreign policy as well as foreign policy considerations in domestic energy policy.

Additional View

We subscribe to the report's analysis and recommendations, but the report understates the gravity of the threat that energy dependence poses to U.S. national security.

Energy is a central challenge to U.S. foreign policy, not simply one of many challenges. Global dependence on oil is rapidly eroding U.S. power and influence because oil is a strategic commodity largely controlled by regressive governments and a cartel that raises prices and multiplies the rents that flow to oil producers. These rents have enriched and emboldened Iran, enabled President Vladamir Putin to undermine Russia's democracy, entrenched regressive autocrats in Africa, forestalled action against genocide in Sudan, and facilitated Venezuela's campaign against free trade in the Americas. Most gravely, oil consumers are in effect financing both sides of the war on terrorism.

Transformation in the use of energy, especially in transportation where oil is unrivaled, in our government's approach to energy research, development, and deployment, and in the way we conduct our foreign policy, is essential. Achieving this transformation requires efforts on at least three fronts.

First, we must integrate energy and foreign policy. For example, we must engage China and India at a presidential level on the impact of their investment practices on regional stability and our common interest in a free market for energy; we must engage Europe on its growing dependence on Russian energy exports and Russia's monopolistic practices. We must also consider asymmetrical means, like support for power and water infrastructure, to compete for political influence in Latin America and Africa.

Second, the United States must expand and deepen the collective energy security system forged by the United States and institutionalized in the International Energy Agency in 1974—not least by bringing China and India into the system. The report endorses this effort but is not sufficiently precise on the best methods; it suggests that the International Energy Forum could be tapped, but that institution is ill-suited as it allows oil producers a veto on its activities.

Third, the United States should use its economic power as a component of its energy strategy. For example, we should consider ways to give preferential access to the U.S. market to producing countries that support a free market in energy. This instrument is blunt and difficult to wield, but among the steps we can take are to make access to energy transportation systems a condition of any new free trade agreement with the United States; limit the ability to access and invest in liquefied natural gas re-gasification facilities on U.S. soil to exporting countries whose markets are also open to U.S. investments; and pursuit of rules to govern fair access and competition within the energy sector as a priority in the next World Trade Organization negotiating round.

All told, an incremental approach to the challenge—as advocated in this report—will not be adequate.

David Goldwyn
Michael Granoff

Task Force Members

Graham T. Allison is Douglas Dillon Professor of Government and Director of the Belfer Center for Science and International Affairs at the John F. Kennedy School of Government. From 1977 to 1989, Dr. Allison served as Dean of the Kennedy School. Dr. Allison has also served as Special Adviser to the Secretary of Defense under President Ronald Reagan and as Assistant Secretary of Defense for Policy and Plans under President Bill Clinton.

Norman R. Augustine retired in 1997 as Chairman and CEO of Lockheed Martin Corporation. Prior to the formation of Lockheed Martin, he had served as Chairman and CEO of the Martin Marietta Corporation since 1987. Formerly, Mr. Augustine served in various posts at the Pentagon, including Undersecretary of the U.S. Army.

Robert A. Belfer is the CEO of Belfer Management LLC, a private investment firm. Mr. Belfer has enjoyed a long career with Belco Petroleum Corporation, where he was named Chairman in 1985. In 1992, Mr. Belfer founded Belco Oil & Gas Corporation, an independent petroleum producer.

Stephen W. Bosworth is the Dean of the Fletcher School of Law and Diplomacy at Tufts University. Dean Bosworth has had an extensive

---

Note: Task Force members participate in their individual and not their institutional capacities.
*The individual has endorsed the report and submitted an additional view.

career in the U.S. Foreign Service, including service as Ambassador to the Republic of Korea, Tunisia, and the Philippines. He also served in a number of senior positions in the Department of State, including Director of Policy Planning.

Helima L. Croft is a Senior Strategist with the Business Intelligence Group at Lehman Brothers. Formerly, she was an Intelligence Fellow at the Council on Foreign Relations. Dr. Croft spent four years at the Central Intelligence Agency, where she was a Senior Economic Analyst in the office of Asian Pacific, Latin American, and African Analysis.

John Deutch, Chair of the Task Force, is an Institute Professor at the Massachusetts Institute of Technology (MIT). Dr. Deutch has been a member of the MIT faculty since 1970, and has served as Chairman of the Department of Chemistry, Dean of Science, and Provost. Dr. Deutch has also served in many senior government posts, including Undersecretary of Energy, Deputy Secretary of Defense, and Director of Central Intelligence.

Charles J. DiBona is the current Chairman of the Sentient Council and retired Chairman of the Board of Logistics Management Institute. Mr. DiBona served nineteen years as President and four years as Executive Vice President with the American Petroleum Institute. Mr. DiBona has also served as a Special Consultant to President Richard Nixon.

Jessica P. Einhorn is Dean of the Paul H. Nitze School of Advanced International Studies at Johns Hopkins University. Dr. Einhorn served a twenty-year career in various positions at the World Bank, including as Managing Director from 1996 to 1998 and as Visiting Fellow at the International Monetary Fund in the wake of the Asian financial crisis.

Martin S. Feldstein is the George F. Baker Professor of Economics at Harvard University and President and CEO of the National Bureau of Economic Research. From 1982 to 1984, Dr. Feldstein was Chairman of the Council of Economic Advisers and Ronald Reagan's Chief

Economic Adviser. He served as President of the American Economic Association in 2004.

David L. Goldwyn* is President of Goldwyn International Strategies. He served as U.S. Assistant Secretary of Energy for International Affairs from 2000 to 2001, and as National Security Deputy to former U.S. Ambassador to the UN Bill Richardson.

Michael D. Granoff* is President and CEO of Pomona Capital, an international private equity investment company. Prior to his business career, Mr. Granoff served on the staff of the U.S. House of Representatives Appropriations Subcommittee on Foreign Operations and on the 1992 Presidential Transition Team at the Department of the Treasury.

J. Bennett Johnston is CEO of Johnston and Associates. Senator Johnston has had a long career in public service, including eight years in the Louisiana legislature and twenty-four years in the U.S. Senate. During his time in the Senate, he served as Chairman of the Senate Committee on Energy and Natural Resources.

Arnold Kanter is a Principal and Founding Member of the Scowcroft Group. Dr. Kanter served as Undersecretary of State from 1991 to 1993 and as Special Assistant to the President from 1989 to 1991, in addition to holding a variety of positions in the State Department.

Karin M. Lissakers serves as Chief Adviser to George Soros on globalization issues at the Soros Fund Management and is Director of the Revenue Watch Institute. Previously, Ms. Lissakers held the post of U.S. Executive Director on the Executive Board of the International Monetary Fund from 1993 to 2001.

Walter E. Massey is President of Morehouse College. Dr. Massey has served as Provost and Senior Vice President for Academic Affairs at the University of California, Vice President for Research at the University of Chicago, Director of the Argonne National Laboratory, and Director of the National Science Foundation.

Ernest J. Moniz is the Cecil and Ida Green Professor of Physics and Engineering Systems and Codirector of the Laboratory for Energy and the Environment at the Massachusetts Institute of Technology, where he has served on the faculty since 1973. Dr. Moniz served as Undersecretary of the Department of Energy from October 1997 to January 2001.

William K. Reilly is Founding Partner of Aqua International Partners. Mr. Reilly is also Cochairman of the National Commission on Energy Policy. He has previously served as the first Payne Visiting Professor at Stanford University, Administrator of the U.S. Environmental Protection Agency, President of the World Wildlife Fund, and President of the Conservation Foundation.

James R. Schlesinger, Chair of the Task Force, is Chairman of the MITRE Corporation and a Senior Adviser at Lehman Brothers. He is also a consultant to the U.S. Department of Defense, a member of the Defense Policy Board, member of the Arms Control Nonproliferation Advisory Board of the Department of State, and a member of the Homeland Security Advisory Council. Dr. Schlesinger formerly served as Secretary of Defense and was the nation's first Secretary of Energy.

Peter Schwartz is Cofounder and Chairman of Global Business Network and a Partner of the Monitor Group. His current research and scenario work encompasses energy resources and the environment, technology, telecommunications, media and entertainment, aerospace, and national security. From 1982 to 1986, Mr. Schwartz headed scenario planning for the Royal Dutch/Shell Group of Companies.

Philip R. Sharp is President of Resources for the Future. His career in public service over the last thirty-five years includes ten terms as a member of the U.S. House of Representatives from Indiana and a lengthy tenure on the faculty of the John F. Kennedy School of Government and the Institute of Politics at Harvard University, where he served as Director.

James B. Steinberg is Dean of the Lyndon B. Johnson School of Public Affairs at the University of Texas at Austin. Previously, he was

Vice President and Director of Foreign Policy Studies at the Brookings Institution. Mr. Steinberg also served as Deputy National Security Adviser to President Bill Clinton, as well as Chief of Staff of the U.S. State Department and Director of the State Department's Policy Planning Staff.

Linda G. Stuntz is a Founding Partner of the law firm of Stuntz, Davis & Staffier, P.C. Her law practice includes energy and environmental regulation, as well as matters relating to government support of technology development and transfer. Previously, Ms. Stuntz served as Deputy Secretary of the U.S. Department of Energy under President George H.W. Bush, and played a principal role in the development and enactment of the Energy Policy Act of 1992.

James L. Sweeney is Director of the Precourt Institute for Energy Efficiency, Professor of Management Science and Engineering at Stanford University, Senior Fellow of the Stanford Institute for Economic Policy Research, and Senior Fellow of the Hoover Institution on War, Revolution, and Peace. He is a Senior Fellow of the U.S. Association for Energy Economics, a Fellow of the California Council on Science and Technology, and a member of Governor Arnold Schwarzenegger's Council of Economic Advisers.

Frank Verrastro is a Senior Fellow and Director of the Energy Program at the Center for Strategic and International Studies. He has also served government staff positions in the White House (Energy Policy and Planning Staff) and the Departments of Interior (Oil and Gas Office) and Energy (Domestic Policy and International Affairs Office), including as Director of the Office of Producing Nations and Deputy Assistant Secretary for International Energy Resources.

David G. Victor, Project Director of the Task Force, is Director of the Program on Energy and Sustainable Development at Stanford University and Adjunct Senior Fellow for Science and Technology at the Council on Foreign Relations. His research focuses on the political economy of energy markets, especially markets for oil, gas, and electricity in developing countries.

J. Robinson West is the Chairman of the Board and Founder of PFC Energy. Previously, Mr. West served in the Reagan administration as Assistant Secretary of the Interior for Policy, Budget, and Administration. He also served in the Ford administration as the Deputy Assistant Secretary of Defense for International Economic Affairs and on the White House Staff.

Task Force Observers

Rachel Bronson
Council on Foreign Relations

Mark A. Bucknam
Council on Foreign Relations

Douglas Holtz-Eakin
Council on Foreign Relations

Charles D. Ferguson
Council on Foreign Relations

Recent Independent Task Force Reports Sponsored by the Council on Foreign Relations

Russia's Wrong Direction: What the United States Can and Should Do (2006); John Edwards and Jack Kemp, Chairs; Stephen Sestanovich, Project Director

More Than Humanitarianism: A Strategic U.S. Approach Toward Africa (2006); Anthony Lake and Christine Todd Whitman, Chairs; Princeton N. Lyman and J. Stephen Morrison, Project Directors

In the Wake of War: Improving U.S. Post-Conflict Capabilities (2005); Samuel R. Berger and Brent Scowcroft, Chairs; William L. Nash, Project Director; Mona K. Sutphen, Deputy Director

In Support of Arab Democracy: Why and How (2005); Madeleine K. Albright and Vin Weber, Chairs; Steven A. Cook, Project Director

Building a North American Community (2005); John P. Manley, Pedro Aspe, and William F. Weld, Chairs; Thomas P. d'Aquino, Andrés Rozental, and Robert A. Pastor, Vice Chairs; Chappel A. Lawson, Project Director; Cosponsored with the Canadian Council of Chief Executives and the Consejo Mexicano de Asuntos Internacionales

Iran: Time for a New Approach (2004); Zbigniew Brzezinski and Robert M. Gates, Chairs; Suzanne Maloney, Project Director

Renewing the Atlantic Partnership (2004); Henry A. Kissinger and Lawrence H. Summers, Chairs; Charles A. Kupchan, Project Director

Nonlethal Weapons and Capabilities (2004); Graham T. Allison and Paul X. Kelley, Chairs; Richard L. Garwin, Project Director

New Priorities in South Asia: U.S. Policy Toward India, Pakistan, and Afghanistan (2003); Frank G. Wisner II, Nicholas Platt, and Marshall M. Bouton, Chairs; Dennis Kux and Mahnaz Ispahani, Project Directors; Cosponsored with the Asia Society

Finding America's Voice: A Strategy for Reinvigorating U.S. Public Diplomacy (2003); Peter G. Peterson, Chair; Jennifer Sieg, Project Director

Emergency Responders: Drastically Underfunded, Dangerously Unprepared (2003); Warren B. Rudman, Chair; Richard A. Clarke, Senior Adviser; Jamie F. Metzl, Project Director

Chinese Military Power (2003); Harold Brown, Chair; Joseph W. Prueher, Vice Chair; Adam Segal, Project Director

Iraq: The Day After (2003); Thomas R. Pickering and James R. Schlesinger, Chairs; Eric P. Schwartz, Project Director

Threats to Democracy (2002); Madeleine K. Albright and Bronislaw Geremek, Chairs; Morton H. Halperin, Project Director; Elizabeth Frawley Bagley, Associate Director

America—Still Unprepared, Still in Danger (2002); Gary Hart and Warren B. Rudman, Chairs; Stephen Flynn, Project Director

Terrorist Financing (2002); Maurice R. Greenberg, Chair; William F. Wechsler and Lee S. Wolosky, Project Directors

Enhancing U.S. Leadership at the United Nations (2002); David Dreier and Lee H. Hamilton, Chairs; Lee Feinstein and Adrian Karatnycky, Project Directors

Testing North Korea: The Next Stage in U.S. and ROK Policy (2001); Morton I. Abramowitz and James T. Laney, Chairs; Robert A. Manning, Project Director

The United States and Southeast Asia: A Policy for the New Administration (2001); J. Robert Kerrey, Chair; Robert A. Manning, Project Director

Strategic Energy Policy: Challenges for the 21ˢᵗ Century (2001); Edward L. Morse, Chair; Amy Myers Jaffe, Project Director

---

All publications listed are available on the Council on Foreign Relations website, CFR.org.
To order printed copies, contact the Brookings Institution Press: 800-537-5487.